S0-ARF-947

COLLECTOR'S
VALUE GUIDE™

Ty® Plush
Animals

Secondary Market Price Guide
& Collector Handbook

SECOND EDITION

Ty® Plush Animals

BEANIE BABIES®, BEANIE BUDDIES®, Ty® and the Ty Heart Logo® are registered trademarks of Ty Inc. BEANIE™, BEANIES™, PILLOW PALS™, ATTIC TREASURES™ and the individual names of each plush animal depicted in this publication are also trademarks of Ty Inc. The plush animals depicted in this publication are the copyrighted property of Ty Inc., and all photographs of Ty Inc.'s products in this publication are used by permission of Ty Inc. ©1999, Ty Inc. The poems associated with Ty Inc.'s BEANIE BABIES plush animals are also the copyrighted property of Ty Inc., and any reproduction of such poems in this publication is with the permission of Ty Inc.

The Collector's Value Guide™ is not sponsored or endorsed by, or otherwise affiliated with Ty Inc. Any opinions expressed are solely those of the authors, and do not necessarily reflect those of Ty Inc. All Copyrights and Trademarks of Ty Inc. are used by permission. All rights reserved.

Front cover (left to right): "Snap™" – *Pillow Pals™,* "Bugsy™" – *Attic Treasures™,* "Smoochy™" – *Beanie Buddies®,* "1999 Signature Bear™" – *Beanie Babies®,* "Scoop™" – *Teenie Beanie Babies™,* "Baby Patches™" – *Ty® Plush*
Back cover (top to bottom): "Harris™" – *Ty® Plush,* "Large Curly™" – *Attic Treasures™,* "Azalea™" – *Attic Treasures™,* "Erin™" – *Beanie Babies®,* "Erin™" – *Beanie Buddies®*

Managing Editor:	Jeff Mahony	Art Director:	Joe T. Nguyen
Associate Editors:	Melissa A. Bennett	Production Supervisor:	Scott Sierakowski
	Jan Cronan	Senior Graphic Designers:	Carole Mattia-Slater
	Gia C. Manalio		Leanne Peters
	Paula Stuckart	Graphic Designers:	Lance Doyle
Contributing Editor:	Mike Micciulla		Sean-Ryan Dudley
Editorial Assistants:	Jennifer Filipek		Kimberly Eastman
	Nicole LeGard Lenderking		Ryan Falis
	Ren Messina		Jason C. Jasch
	Joan C. Wheal		David S. Maloney
Research Assistants:	Priscilla Berthiaume		David Ten Eyck
	Beth Hackett		
	Victoria Puorro		
	Steven Shinkaruk		

ISBN 1-888914-50-5

CHECKERBEE™ and COLLECTOR'S VALUE GUIDE™ are trademarks of CheckerBee, Inc.

Copyright© by CheckerBee, Inc. 1999. All rights reserved. No part of this book may be reproduced or transmitted in any form or by any means, electronic or mechanical, including photocopying, recording, or by any information storage or retrieval system, without the written permission of the publisher.

CheckerBee PUBLISHING

(formerly Collectors' Publishing)
306 Industrial Park Road • Middletown, CT 06457

collectorbee.com

TABLE OF CONTENTS

TABLE OF CONTENTS

Introducing The Collector's Value Guide™

*W*elcome to the second edition of the Collector's Value Guide™ to Ty® Plush Animals! Today these bags of beans and stuffing can be found almost everywhere from hiding in a child's bedroom toy box to riding on a car dashboard to sitting beside a computer monitor. Our easy-to-use, reliable and comprehensive guide will be the only resource that you will ever need to direct you through the wilds of your Ty plush animals collecting adventure.

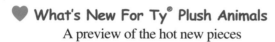

Read All About It!

Here you will discover the most accurate and up-to-date information on all of your favorite Ty collectibles, including *Attic Treasures™*, *Beanie Babies®*, *Beanie Buddies®*, *Teenie Beanie Babies™*, *Pillow Pals™* and *Ty® Plush*!

Ty® Plush Animals Overview ♥
A look at the entire Ty family

♥ What's New For Ty® Plush Animals
A preview of the hot new pieces

Odds & Ends ♥
A spotlight on some of the unique features of Ty plush animals

♥ Swing Tags & Tush Tags
An examination of the different
tag generations and their significance

Value Guide ♥
Full-color photos of every piece in the line along with
vital statistics including size, animal type, style number,
issue date and status (current or retired), as well as
1999 secondary market value

Ty® Plush Animals Overview

W hen Ty Warner began his entrepreneurial adventure in the wilderness of plush animals, he knew that the industry was more than just a bunch of stuffing. However, little did he know that his company, Ty Inc., would become the multi-million dollar corporate leader that it has become today or that he, himself, would become such an icon.

Warner was no stranger to the world of plush and, as an employee for Dakin, he made his mark in this world long before forming his own company. A natural salesman, Warner would arrive at a potential client's office in a Rolls Royce and dressed in a fur coat and top hat. From that point on, the center stage would become his. Yet, other ambitions were calling and in the early 1980s, Warner quit his job so that he could travel overseas.

But the call of the plush was strong and after a few years, Warner returned to the United States and in 1986, he established his very own toy company with the birth of a small litter of life-like cats and a couple of canines. In the introductory letter to retailers from the 1989 catalog, the company stated its mission: "We are committed to be the best . . . The Very Best." And while Ty Inc. did well its first years, it wasn't exactly a huge overnight success. However, Warner and his employees stuck to their mission and their attention to detail and quality paid off. The rest is history.

While people are probably most familiar with the *Beanie Babies* (let's face it, you'll pretty much see these little critters anywhere you turn), the other Ty lines have also made quite a name for themselves. Many people have discovered that the well loved bears, cats and dogs, as well as a variety of other critters, that have been sitting on their shelves or maybe up in the attic for many years, are actually members of the Ty family. Over the years, the Ty family tree has blossomed to over 600 pieces. And, in 1993, in an effort to reach more people and expand his growing business, Warner introduced *The Attic Treasures Collection*. The *Beanie Babies* were born in 1994 and *The Pillow Pals Collection* in 1995. At this time, it seemed like there was a bit of Ty Inc. everywhere and just when people may have thought that there couldn't be anymore, Warner surprised everyone by teaming up with McDonald's fast-food restaurants to offer a *Teenie Beanie Babies* promotion in 1997 and again in 1998. Then in 1998, Ty took another big step and introduced *Beanie Buddies*, larger, mirror-images of the now famous *Beanies*.

THE LOOK OF LOVE

Attic Treasures is a collection of fully jointed characters that have been through a variety of stylish changes over the years. Designed in the manner of old-fashioned, well-loved, humpbacked bears of days gone by, these pieces offer a bit of nostalgia for the young and the old(er).

The first of the collection was a menagerie of twelve bears and rabbits between 6 and 12 inches tall. Originally known as *The Attic Treasures Collection*, this grouping's name was changed to "Ty Collectibles" in 1995 and was known as such until reverting back to its original name in 1998.

The collection also underwent a very obvious physical change: many members of the clan began to wear clothes. In the early years, the characters chose to be "bare" or to sport only a ribbon. However, as time went on, they became more fashion-conscious and began appearing in a variety of outfits including dresses and overalls. Some of the *Attic Treasures* have even changed their outfits during their lifetime.

TY® PLUSH ANIMALS OVERVIEW

Until 1993, the names of the individual designers of Ty plush animals were not publicized, leading to the assumption that Warner himself was the sole designer. However, in an effort to add diversity to the style of his animals for his new collection, Warner enlisted the help of Canadian teddy bear artists Linda Harris and Ruth Fraser. Shortly thereafter, Nola Hart and Anne Nickles joined the creative team and the names of the various artists began to appear printed on their creations' swing tags.

IT'S A BEAN-FILLED WORLD, BABY

When Ty introduced nine beanbag critters called *Beanie Babies* at a Chicago area trade fair in late 1993, no one could have imagined the furor that would follow. Sure, they were adorable and priced so that just about anyone could afford them, but these tiny, modest characters hardly seemed to foreshadow that they were about to become giants in the world of collectibles.

The phenomenon began in 1995 when the first three *Beanies* were retired, giving them a status that would catapult the line into the realm of the serious collectible. It was all a whirlwind from that point on as the *Beanies* became the hottest craze to hit the market in a long time.

However, the *Beanie Babies* haven't just sat around and let the success go to their heads. In the midst of this frenzy, these characters have done a lot of good. In 1997, many participated in an extremely prosperous effort to increase attendance at a variety of sporting events, as they were handed out to children attendees.

Others have lent their efforts as fundraising incentives such as "Maple" who helped promote awareness for the Canadian Special Olympics, as well as "Princess" whose profits helped raise over $8 million dollars for the Diana, Princess of Wales Memorial Fund.

And one thing for sure is that these characters are not afraid of the being in the spotlight. Since their debut, *Beanies* have shown up just about everywhere from television programs to The Sporting News magazine's list of the 100 most powerful people in sports for 1998 where "Glory" appeared among such icons as Michael Jordan. Also, anyone who has surfed the Internet will know that the presence of *Beanie Babies* is almost overwhelming.

Sometimes Size Does Count

"Wow, it's almost like looking in a mirror." That's how you may feel when you see the *Beanie Buddies*, larger counterparts to the *Beanie Babies*. *Beanie Buddies* are made from a special material called "Tylon." Reportedly designed by Ty Warner himself, this material is made to be extra soft and cool. These characters made their debut in Fall 1998, but almost immediately they became very difficult to track down in retail stores. Ty Inc. explained on its web site in late 1998 that because the creation of Tylon is a slow process, they wouldn't be able to ship any more *Beanie Buddies* for a short while.

The shortage of *Beanie Buddies* helped create a lot of collector interest in the new line. The original *Beanie Buddies* clan consisted of nine designs, and were joined by 14 more in 1999. The very first *Beanie Buddies* retirement occurred in December 1998 when "Twigs" was honored with that status, only to be joined by "Beak" in early 1999.

Ty® Plush Animals Overview

♥ Not Exactly
A Teenie Appetite

In April 1997, Ty joined forces with the fast-food giant McDonald's for a promotion that would cause cravings for burgers like never before and leave many fans hungry. The promotion featured 10 tiny replicas of *Beanie Babies* which were packaged in special bags and packed into Happy Meals (which also came in *Beanie*-themed bags). This promotion was so successful that, in less than a month, everything was sold out and it was over.

Inspired by this success, McDonald's decided to do it again in May 1998. This time, 12 new designs were issued but the response was just as great, causing them to sell out once again in a very short time. In fact, not only were people starving for the actual *Teenie Beanies Babies*, they were feeding on anything they could get their hands on, including the promotional posters and buttons worn by McDonald's employees during the event. This added new meaning to the question, "Do you want fries with that?"

☾ Bigger, Softer,
Brighter

In an effort to extend its appeal even further, Ty introduced a line of infant-friendly characters called *Pillow Pals*. Designed to resemble their *Beanie* cousins, these machine washable pals were made with embroidered eyes and noses that were resistant to being torn off by the little hands they were created for.

This season has brought about a brilliant change in the collection. The once pastel critters have been taken out of production and re-introduced in strong, vibrant colors. For example, "Antlers" the moose traded in his brown fur and orange antlers for a bright green body and purple and yellow antlers (and even orange and yellow nostrils!). The cream and brown "Meow," who had experienced a change of fur once before, now finally decided on a radiant purple coat with blue and yellow ears and green paws.

This change was brought about by the theory that small children like bright colors. And as Ty is well known for doing things in extremes, the introduction of pieces of this color is no exception.

LIONS AND TIGERS AND BEARS AND UNICORNS...

The *Ty Plush* collection has come a long way since the very first litter of cats and dogs. This small grouping of animals has turned into a menagerie of over 300 items, unfortunately the majority of which have been retired (though most were taken out of production long before Ty began to use the official "retirement" term) and are no longer available in regular retail outlets. However, with Ty's prolific releases over several years, many people may actually be the lucky owners of these pieces and not even know it.

Without any sense of organization, the plush collection would be quite a zoo. So to make it much more manageable, Ty divides these critters into five distinct categories:

BEARS: This category makes up the largest grouping in the plush animal collection. For over 10 years, these bruins have been a part of the Ty family tree.

Ty® Plush Animals Overview

CATS: From the very beginning, cats have been a major part of the Ty family tree. As the collection has grown, so has the diversity as tabbies and calicos, among others, have joined the original Himalayans.

DOGS: Also part of the collection from the very beginning, this category of canines has really expanded with a variety of breeds and designs since its early days.

COUNTRY: This grouping features a variety of animals fresh off the farm. Here you will find cows, horses, lambs, of course pigs and even a fantastic unicorn.

WILDLIFE: It really is a jungle out there and in this grouping, you will find all kinds of wild things from monkeys to panthers.

Movin' Right Along

So what's next for Ty Inc.? While no one knows for sure, the one thing that we can all be sure of is Ty's tremendous ability to surprise us. And the company creativity (and therefore, success) shows no signs of slowing down. So all we can do is wait and see, but in the meantime, we can enjoy all of the wonderful lines now offered by Ty.

*O*n January 1, 1999, Ty Inc. released a total of 66 new animals featuring innovative color combinations and designs. Let's start with the introductions!

Attic Treasures™

Twelve new pieces joined this group, along with five former *Ty Plush* pieces who donned sweaters with patriotic and spring motifs for the 1999 season.

AZALEA™

This lovely "Azalea," a lavender lop-eared bunny, is anxious for spring to arrive and would be an attractive addition to an Easter basket or springtime display. Her tag warns: "Hare Today – Gone Tomorrow!" so pick up this one before she hops away!

BEEZEE™

Flower blossoms won't stand a chance with this little "buzzer" flying around! Dressed in a bumble bee costume, "Beezee" is sure to makes a beeline right into your heart with the statement: "You BEE-long to Me!"

BUGSY™

"Always A Lady," "Bugsy" masquerades as an unassuming ladybug, hoping to charm you with her original fashion sense.

CAMELIA™

This peach of a southern belle bunny is "Always In Bloom!" and can add a colorful dimension to your spring decor. "Camelia" is sporting a lovely ribbon which is the perfect complement to her pastel fur.

"How Does Your Garden Grow?" is the question on the mind of this crow. "Cawley" is dressed in his denim overalls and straw hat, ready for a day in the cornfield.

CAWLEY™

BABY CURLY™

CURLY™

LARGE CURLY™

CLIMBING UP TO THE ATTIC

Formerly members of the *Ty Plush* collection, these "Curly" pals have not only had a change of wardrobe, but also a change of scenery, as they now call *The Attic Treasures Collection* their humble abode.

These All-American bears have marched into the collection in a very nationalistic way as each dons a sweater adorned with the symbols of their country. "Baby Curly" the bear looks like a proud little patriot in his "USA" sweater, while his brothers "Curly" and "Large Curly" display their pride on their sweaters which are adorned with the flag.

And both the tan "Curly Bunny" and the white "Curly Bunny" spring into the collection with sweaters adorned with the fruits (and vegetables) of the season.

CURLY BUNNY™

CURLY BUNNY™

WHAT'S NEW FOR TY® PLUSH ANIMALS

As children, we often heard this line at the end of many fairy tales: "And They Lived Happily Ever After!" This little goose "Georgette" (could it be "Mother," herself?) reminds us that all bedtime stories should have happy endings.

GEORGETTE™

GEORGIA™

"Georgia" looks like she got her paws a bit too deep into the Easter egg paint! She is covered with a colorful assortment of paint strokes and is holding a flowered egg for your Easter basket.

Although "Into Each Life A Little Rain Must Fall," "Gordon" is prepared for a downpour in his bright yellow slicker and rain hat. He is the perfect reminder that rainbows appear when you least expect it and that the sun will always shine through the darkest clouds.

GORDON™

HEARTLEY™

Instead of wearing his heart on his sleeve, "Heartley" wears his on the front of his sweater and proclaims "Love Conquers All!" This bruin boasts a more subdued color scheme than many of his peers with the gold and maroon accents, which inspired his name.

RADCLIFFE™

Always the rascally raccoon, "Radcliffe" is not shy about being known as the "Thief Of Hearts!" He is ready to steal your heart and hold it captive the minute you catch sight of him with his masked eyes and scruffy fur!

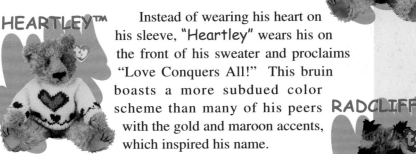

WHAT'S NEW FOR TY® PLUSH ANIMALS

RAMSEY™

Perhaps you can help this "Little Lamsadivy!" find some ivy to eat (remember the old ditty, "Mairzy Doats?"). "Ramsey" is poking around the yard looking for her favorite snack and would love to find a home with you!

SKYLAR™

"The Sky Is The Limit!" for this sweet bear who is dressed in a cozy sky blue colored sweater, waiting for the first hint of spring! But, alas! "Skylar" is really headed for the outer limits – he was quickly retired on March 31, 1999!

1999 SIGNATURE BEAR™

BEANIE BABIES®

Everyone wants Ty Warner's autograph – and here is the bear that provides just that! "1999 Signature Bear" has a facsimile of Warner's signature stitched onto the familiar red heart found on this bear's chest. A special bear, indeed, for Ty bear enthusiasts!

We all have our favorites and this pooch is sure to be one of them. While his name may sound "ruff," "Butch" is nothing but a real softie, waiting patiently for his master to bring him a treat and scratch behind his ear.

BUTCH™

EGGBERT™

A shy chick, "Eggbert" pops in (actually, out) just in time for spring. She prefers to stay in her shell which makes it very convenient to play her favorite game, hide and seek!

COLLECTOR'S
VALUE GUIDE™

What's New For Ty® Plush Animals

EWEY™

Another design which was released to coincide with the spring season, "Ewey," the lamb, quietly ushers in the season.

With luxurious fur and a royal blue bow around his neck, "Fuzz" gives all who sees him that warm and fuzzy feeling. He may have an everyday name, but this handsome bear will add "class, style and flair" to your den of bears!

FUZZ™

GERMANIA™

Available exclusively in Germany, "Germania" proudly bears her nation's flag on her chest. She is slowly making her way around the world, due to the love of Ty collectors who are tracking down this addition for their *Beanie Babies* family.

GOATEE™

As the collection's first goat, "Goatee" climbs onto the scene with pride as one of the few chosen to be included as a sports promotion *Beanie Baby*!

GOOCHY™

This multi-colored, tentacled jellyfish must be extremely ticklish with a name like "Goochy!" He was tickled pink (and blue and green and yellow!) to be chosen as the official Ty web site "Info Beanie" for March 1999!

HIPPIE™

Another "ty"-dyed animal appears this year in the form of this colorful bunny named "Hippie." This retro rabbit will dance and twirl his way into your heart.

What's New For Ty® Plush Animals

HOPE™

With closed eyes and folded hands, "Hope" is the perfect friend to say a prayer with at the end of the day. And what would be better to cuddle up under the covers with than a little "hope?"

KICKS™

Capitalizing on the ever-growing popularity of soccer, sporty "Kicks" runs onto the field and he's ready to rumble!

LUKE™

Lovable "Luke" adds a little class to the dog pound with his perky black and white gingham bow. How can you resist those eyes?

MAC™

It will be hard to miss "Mac" soaring into the line with his bright red coat and the stylish tuft of hair on his head. However, he's sure to ruffle some collector's feathers as this colorful cardinal will be flying quickly off store shelves.

MILLENIUM™

One of the special *Beanie Babies* to be issued on the same day as her birth date, the cuddly "Millenium" is looking forward to her first birthday party, New Year's Day, 2000!

MOOCH™

His name has caused this spider monkey a lot of grief but "Mooch" just wants to call somewhere his home. He promises to behave himself and always say "please" and "thank you," and the only thing he'll want to mooch is your love and attention.

WHAT'S NEW FOR TY® PLUSH ANIMALS

NIBBLY™

NIBBLER™

"Nibbler" and "Nibbly" . . . The "Nibble" siblings arrived together this year and are sure to multiply at your house – as bunnies often do! They are quite a pair with their wiggly noses and perky ears – always on the lookout for a quick "nibble" and a place to call a hutch of their own. Could it be with the rest of your Ty bunnies?

PRICKLES™

Imitating a pincushion is the forte of this pleasant pal "Prickles." She would love to keep you company while you are darning those socks (does anyone do that anymore?!)

SAMMY™

"Sammy" the tie-dyed bear is the latest in a prestigious line of "lay-flat" *Beanie Baby* bears, joining such luminaries as the retired "Chilly" and "Peking." With his beautiful pastel colors, "Sammy" will add a feeling of happiness into any collection.

SCAT™

A newborn kitten who can barely stand on her own four feet, "Scat" scampers in to replace old-timers "Pounce" and "Prance," who both retired on March 31, 1999.

SLIPPERY™

If you rescue the friendly seal "Slippery" from the frigid ocean waters, you can show him how to surf the net instead of getting caught in one! This mustachioed marine animal can relax with his pals and "carp" about the fish that got away!

WHAT'S NEW FOR TY® PLUSH ANIMALS

STILTS™

Do you know an expectant mom waiting for her bundle of joy to arrive? "Stilts," the stork, would be the perfect surprise for both mother and child.

TINY™

A hot tamale on legs, "Tiny" is just waiting to put a little spice in your life! Bring him home and let the festivities begin!

VALENTINA™

This year's valentine teddy will make your heart skip a beat and ensure that your true love will last forever – in the form of "Valentina." She makes the perfect addition to any collection that also includes her close friend and confidante – the recently retired "Valentino."

BEANIE BUDDIES®

Making their debut last fall, the *Beanie Buddies* add 14 new designs this year, all of them larger versions of current and retired *Beanie Babies*.

BONGO™

"Bongo" is not monkeying around! He wants to hang around at your house and show the rest of his jungle buddies how to make his favorite dessert – banana splits, of course! Better stock up on the ice cream!

BUBBLES™

Making a bold fashion statement, "Bubbles" is one buddy that will be hard to miss on any store shelf! Her bright yellow and black stripes make her quite attractive to all collectors wishing to reel her in!

WHAT'S NEW FOR TY® PLUSH ANIMALS

Special care will keep this pure white beauty keep looking his best. "Chilly" is quite willing to take it easy and keep his paws clean just to have the chance to warm up to you.

CHILLY™

CHIP™

This kitty is a "Chip" off the old Ty block with her look-a-like *Beanie Babies* version. Their calico pattern is a charmer among the kitty connoisseurs!

ERIN™

"Erin" is one way to proudly proclaim your Emerald Isle ancestry or just to invite the luck of the Irish into your collection! He is yet another bear with international flair!

HIPPITY™

"Hippity" could be waiting in your basket to surprise you on Easter morning. Considering his size, he could actually hand you your eggs and marshmallow chicks!

PATTI™

By now, every child can recognize a platypus, with five versions now in the Ty family! "Patti" is the *Buddy*-sized version to complete your collection.

PEKING™

With Ty branching out to include animals with an international theme, "Peking" represents the lovable bamboo-munching bears native to the continent of Asia.

What's New For Ty® Plush Animals

"Pinky's" elegant neck and stately stature puts this warm weather buddy "head and shoulders" above the rest!

PINKY™

SMOOCHY™ So, how many frogs will you have to kiss to end up with your prince? Only one – as long as you start with this handsome guy, "Smoochy!"

The only thing "bull-ish" about this *Beanie Buddy* is "Snort's" vibrant red coat which collectors seem to "(mat)adore!"

SNORT™

SQUEALER™ This little porker promises to clean up his act if only "Squealer" can join your buddy barnyard!

You won't have to worry about losing your valuables with "Tracker," the professional sniffer around! Don't let those innocent, puppy-dog eyes fool you, this pooch "nose" what's going on.

TRACKER™

WADDLE™

Bringing a little class to the *Buddy* set, "Waddle" put on his best duds and brought up the rear (alphabetically, that is) – of the new *Beanie Buddies* for 1999!

WHAT'S NEW FOR TY® PLUSH ANIMALS

PILLOW PALS™

The new introductions in the *Pillow Pals* collection this year are a bright set of animals with choices in fur color that can only be found in our imaginations! Let's take a peek at these wild ones:

ANTLERS™

Where else but in Ty-land could you find a green moose with one purple antler and one yellow antler? "Antlers" may find it hard to get dressed in the morning but everyone can see him coming!

BA BA™

This little lamb may be shy, but "Ba Ba" is passionate about her new purple coat!

CARROTS™

They say you are what you eat and "Carrots" has eaten so many of her favorite vegetables that her ears and nose have turned a bright shade of orange!

CHEWY™

"Chewy," the busy fellow at the neighborhood dam is sure to open the floodgates of love in his turquoise coat and prominent incisors!

HUGGY™

Our friendly "Huggy" is brighter than the average bear with his lemon yellow body and bright red ears! Better watch out for the surprise squeezes he loves to give to his favorite pals!

What's New For Ty® Plush Animals

KOLALA™

Check out the ears on this "bloke from down under!" "Kolala" is ready to catch up on all of the pal gossip and his ears are waiting to catch up on all of the news!

MEOW™

"Meow" won't be able to pussyfoot around with her eye-catching color combination of pink, green, yellow and blue! Whew!

PADDLES™

Just to be a little different, "Paddles" chose a lime green ensemble to wear instead of the fuchsia-colored outfits worn by her platypus friends in other Ty collections!

RIBBIT™

Taking a hint from the business world, "Ribbit" is sporting his bright red "power ty" all over his body! Taking a hint from the head "Ty" guy himself, huh?

RUSTY™

In an effort to get away from the "mask" image, "Rusty" the raccoon came up with a lovely combination of yellow, orange and brown to camouflage the rings around his eyes. Perhaps a nap would eliminate those bags!

SHERBET™

"Sherbet" liked the "ty-dyed" effect so he just put a twinkle in his eyes and stayed with the sure thing!

WHAT'S NEW FOR TY® PLUSH ANIMALS

"Snap" may be a little slowpoke, but he was quick to accept his brand new colorful shell and was first at the finish line with his purple and green feet!

SNAP™

Taking a hiatus from the circus circuit, "Squirt" is looking forward to a little respite with the rest of his *Pillow Pals.* And the break seems to be doing him good – he's just glowing.

SQUIRT™

This "true blue" friend will hang around your tree house forever if you let him! "Swinger" will cause a fever in your collection's jungle!

SWINGER™

"Woof'" is one peach of a puppy! You won't be able to resist his droopy, poochy pair of eyes! This one is sure to be another favorite with *Pillow Pal* fans!

WOOF™

TY® PLUSH

"Baby Patches" is honored to be the sole newborn in the *Ty Plush* family this season. Mama "Patches" couldn't be more pleased with her "spittin' image" and the rest of the dogs at Ty are welcoming the puppy into the pound.

BABY PATCHES™

COLLECTORS' CLUB NEWS

*D*ue to the immense popularity of its *Beanie Babies*, Ty Inc. created the company's first collectors' club expressly for *Beanie Babies* fans.

Developed in conjunction with Cyrk Inc. – a promotional marketing company based in Gloucester, Mass. – the Beanie Babies Official Club (B.B.O.C.) made its debut in March 1998 and sparked a new flurry of collecting activity as club members scrambled to obtain the club's first members-only bear, "Clubby."

"Clubby" and the first edition Gold Charter Membership Kits officially retired in March 1999 to make way for the new 1999 Platinum kits and the club's new exclusive bear. Available in the spring of 1999 through authorized Ty retailers designated as B.B.O.C. Headquarters, the new Platinum kits were produced with a suggested retail price of $20 and come with the following:

- B.B.O.C. Exclusive Bear
- Membership Certificate
- Newsletter
- Platinum Set of Beanie Cards
- Platinum Collector Coin
- Pocket Checklist

INSTANT SUCCESS

- Millions of people joined the B.B.O.C. during the club's first four months.

- The B.B.O.C. received hundreds of thousands of orders for "Clubby" even before collectors knew what the piece was going to look like!

- In 1999, First Edition Gold Charter Members will receive special B.B.O.C. mailings as well as any special "For Gold Charter Members Only" offers.

*T*y Inc. has retired 110 pieces between December 31, 1998 and March 31, 1999, including 10 *Attic Treasures*, 43 *Beanie Babies*, 2 *Beanie Buddies*, 21 *Pillow Pals* and 34 *Ty Plush* pieces. Following is a list of these pieces with their animal type, style number and issue year.

ATTIC TREASURES™

RETIRED 3/31/99
Casanova™ (bear, #6073, 1998)
Skylar™ (bear, #6096, 1999)

RETIRED 12/31/98
Esmerelda™ (bear, #6086, 1998)
Gem™ (bear, #6107, 1998)
Iris™ (rabbit, #6077, 1998)
Ivy™ (rabbit, #6076, 1998)

Jangle™ (bear, #6082, 1998)
Laurel™ (bear, #6081, 1998)
Peter™ (bear, #6084, 1998)
Rose™ (rabbit, #6078, 1998)

BEANIE BABIES®

RETIRED 3/31/99
Batty™ (bat, #4035, 1997)
Chip™ (cat, #4121, 1997)
Gobbles™ (turkey, #4034, 1997)
Hissy™ (snake, #4185, 1997)

Iggy™ (iguana, #4038, 1997)
Mel™ (bear, #4162, 1997)
Nanook™ (husky, #4104, 1997)
Pouch™ (kangaroo, #4161, 1997)

RECENT RETIREMENTS

Pounce™ (cat, #4122, 1997)
Prance™ (cat, #4123, 1997)
Pugsly™ (pug dog, #4106, 1997)
Rainbow™ (chameleon, #4037, 1997)
Smoochy™ (frog, #4039, 1997)

Spunky™ (cocker spaniel, #4184,1997)
Stretch™ (ostrich, #4182, 1997)
Strut™ (rooster, #4171, 1997)
RETIRED 3/15/99
Clubby™ (bear, N/A, 1998)

RETIRED 12/31/98
1998 Holiday Teddy™
(bear, #4204, 1998)
Ants™ (anteater, #4195, 1998)
Bongo™ (monkey, #4067, 1995)
Chocolate™ (moose, #4015, 1994)

Claude™ (crab, #4083, 1997)
Congo™ (gorilla, #4160, 1996)
Curly™ (bear, #4052, 1996)
Doby™ (Doberman, #4110, 1997)
Dotty™ (Dalmatian, #4100, 1997)
Fetch™ (golden retriever, #4189, 1998)

Fleece™ (lamb, #4125, 1997)
Freckles™ (leopard, #4066, 1996)
Glory™ (bear, #4188, 1998)
Nuts™ (squirrel, #4114, 1997)
Pinky™ (flamingo, #4072, 1995)

Pumkin'™ (pumpkin, #4205, 1998)
Roary™ (lion, #4069, 1997)
Santa™ (elf, #4203, 1998)
Scoop™ (pelican, #4107, 1996)
Snip™ (Siamese cat, #4120, 1997)

RECENT RETIREMENTS

Spike™ (rhinoceros, #4060, 1996)
Stinger™ (scorpion, #4193, 1998)
Tuffy™ (terrier, #4108, 1997)
Valentino™ (bear, #4058, 1995)
Wise™ (owl, #4187, 1998)
Zero™ (penguin, #4207, 1998)

BEANIE BUDDIES®

RETIRED 3/31/99
Beak™ (kiwi, #9301, 1998)
RETIRED 12/31/98
Twigs™ (giraffe, #9308, 1998)

PILLOW PALS™

RETIRED 12/31/98
Antlers™ (moose, #3028, 1998)
Ba Ba™ (lamb, #3008, 1997)
Bruiser™ (bulldog, #3018, 1997)
Carrots™ (bunny, #3010, 1997)

Clover™ (rabbit, #3020, 1998)
Foxy™ (fox, #3022, 1998)
Glide™ (porpoise, #3025, 1998)
Meow™ (cat, #3011, 1997)

Moo™ (cow, #3004, 1995)
Oink™ (pig, #3005, 1995)
Paddles™ (platypus, #3026, 1998)
Red™ (bull, #3021, 1998)

Ribbit™ (frog, #3009, 1997)
Sherbet™ (bear, #3027, 1998)
Speckles™ (leopard, #3017, 1997)
Spotty™ (Dalmatian, #3019, 1998)

Squirt™ (elephant, #3013, 1997)
Swinger™ (monkey, #3023, 1998)
Tide™ (whale, #3024, 1998)
Tubby™ (hippo, #3012, 1997)
Woof™ (dog, #3003, 1995)

Recent Retirements

Ty® Plush

RETIRED 12/31/98

Baby Ginger™ (bear, #5108, 1997)
Baby Paws™ (bear, #5112, 1998)
Baby PJ™ (bear, #5016, 1993)
Baby Powder™ (bear, #5109, 1997)
Bamboo™ (bear, #5113, 1998)

Cocoa™ (bear, #5107, 1997)
Forest™ (bear, #5114, 1998)
Hope™ (bear, #5601, 1996)
Jumbo PJ™ (bear, #9020, 1992)
Large PJ™ (bear, #9012, 1992)

Papa PJ™ (bear, #9021, 1997)
PJ™ (bear, #5400, 1991)
Al E. Kat™ (cat, #1112, 1989)
Angel™ (cat, #1122, 1998)
Licorice™ (cat, #1125, 1998)

Maggie™ (cat, #1115, 1992)
Ace™ (dog, #2027, 1998)
Elvis™ (dog, #2010, 1995)
Honey™ (dog, #2001, 1995)
Muffin™ (dog, #2020, 1996)

Sherlock™ (dog, #2029, 1998)
Sunny™ (dog, #2028, 1998)
Timber™ (dog, #2002, 1994)
Jersey™ (country, #8026, 1997)
Tulip™ (country, #8008,1996)

Baby George™ (wildlife, #7300, 1996)
Freddie™ (wildlife, #8010, 1991)
Leo™ (wildlife, #7427, 1997)
Mango™ (wildlife, #7100, 1995)
Mango™ (wildlife, #7102, 1995)

Mortimer™ (wildlife, #7417, 1996)
Tango™ (wildlife, #7000, 1995)
Tango™ (wildlife, #7002, 1995)
Tygger™ (wildlife, #7420, 1991)

*U*pon entering the world of Ty plush animals, one is never sure exactly what to expect. It's hardly a world of quiet stuffed animals sitting on a shelf – it's a zoo out there. Take a look:

WHAT TYPE OF RETIREMENT PLAN IS THIS? IT'S A LOT OF WORK!

Once again, Ty made recent retirements a very interactive process as visitors to the official Ty web site (www.ty.com) met the challenge of playing a game in order to discover the pieces that faced surprise retirement on March 31, 1999. Similar to "The Memory Game," players had to click on each window which would open up to reveal an animal. Finding two of the same meant that the piece would be retired. Over the course of three days, two *Attic Treasures*, 16 *Beanie Babies* and one *Beanie Buddy* retired.

THE RELEASES ARE SO BRIGHT... INFANTS GOTTA WEAR SHADES

The newest *Pillow Pals* releases may cause you to have a glowing sense of déjà vu. Their names are familiar and their designs are familiar, but these are definitely not the *Pillow Pals* you used to know. Designed for infants, these critters were stuffed to be extra soft and sported embroidered eyes and noses that couldn't be removed by little hands (or big hands). They were also machine-washable because those little hands could get into a whole lot of dirt. And now, in what seems to be a change of heart (or that would be fur), Ty has stopped production of the pastel versions of these pals and has released them in new, vibrant colors. All this is an attempt to create animals that are even more infant-friendly as most child psychologists will tell you that small children love bright colors. So it's no doubt that these infants are sure to love these *Pillow Pals*!

Ty® Plush Odds & Ends

Ask Not What Your Country Can Do For You...

There seems to be a growing trend within Ty towards releasing special characters that are exclusive to a particular country and who show their allegiance and sense of unity by sporting the symbolic flag of their region. "Germania," a German exclusive *Beanie Baby,* joined his exotic friends, the British "Britannia" and the Canadian "Maple" as a world-traveling collectible. Recently, the *Attic Treasures* line decided to expand its horizons and the nationalistic "Jack" and "Mackenzie" became available only in the U.K. and Canada, respectively.

But these exclusives aren't the only characters showing a sense of patriotism. *Beanie Babies* "Glory," "Libearty," "Lefty" and "Righty" all sport the American flag on their fur and *Attic Treasures* "Baby Curly" and "Grant" are among others who have recently put on sweaters designed with a patriotic theme.

Will The Defendant Please Approach The Stand?

Sure, they look innocent enough, but it seems like no matter which newspaper you pick up or what news program you tune into, you'll discover one of those little *Beanie Babies* causing trouble. In fact, one possibly counterfeit *Beanie Baby* caused so many problems that it found itself in a dispute which aired on the court television program "Judge Judy."

And when the truth finally "fluttered" into the legal chambers, it turned out to be an unhappy verdict for the fake bag of beans.

ATTIC TREASURES™ TOP FIVE

*T*his section showcases the five most valuable pieces in the *Attic Treasures* collection as determined by their secondary market values. All of the values listed are for Generation 1 swing tags only and some of the pieces listed are variations of the original piece. For more information about these interesting secondary market factors, see the *Variations* section on page 218 and *Swing Tags* on page 224.

WOOLIE™ (#6011)
Issued 1993 - Retired 1993
Secondary Market Value: ♥-$1,200

HENRY™ (#6005)
Issued 1993 - Retired 1997
Blue Ribbon/Gold Version
Secondary Market Value: ♥-$1,100

REGGIE™ (#6004)
Issued 1993 - Retired 1995
Red Ribbon Version
Secondary Market Value: ♥-$570
Navy Ribbon Version
Secondary Market Value: ♥-$475

CLIFFORD™ (#6003)
Issued 1993 - Retired 1995
Secondary Market Value: ♥-$380

GILBERT™ (#6015)
Issued 1993 - Retired 1993
Secondary Market Value: ♥-$370

Beanie Babies® Top Five

*T*his section showcases the five most valuable *Beanie Babies* as determined by their secondary market values. Many of the pieces listed here were released for a very limited time (or were not made available to the general public) causing them to be more coveted and therefore more valuable on the secondary market.

#1 BEAR™ (N/A)
Exclusive Ty Sales Representative Gift
Issued December 11-14, 1998
Secondary Market Value:
Special Tag – $10,000

PEANUT™ (#4062)
Dark Blue Version
Issued 1995 - Retired 1998
Secondary Market Value: ❸- $4,800

BROWNIE™ (#4010)
Issued 1994 - Retired 1994
Secondary Market Value: ❶- $4,100

NANA™ (#4067)
Issued 1995 - Retired 1995
Secondary Market Value: ❸- $4,050

TEDDY™ (VIOLET, #4055)
New Face/Employee Bear w/Red Tush Tag
Issued 1994 - Retired 1996
Secondary Market Value:
No Swing Tag – $4,000

TEENIE BEANIE BABIES™ TOP FIVE

*T*his section showcases the five most valuable *Teenie Beanie Babies* as determined by their secondary market values. While the secondary market is active for all *Teenie Beanie Babies*, pieces that were available early in the first promotion are generally the most valuable.

PINKY™
1st Promotion, #2
Issued 1997 - Retired 1997
Secondary Market Value: $45

PATTI™
1st Promotion, #1
Issued 1997 - Retired 1997
Secondary Market Value: $36

CHOPS™
1st Promotion, #3
Issued 1997 - Retired 1997
Secondary Market Value: $32

CHOCOLATE™
1st Promotion, #4
Issued 1997 - Retired 1997
Secondary Market Value: $30

SEAMORE™
1st Promotion, #7
Issued 1997 - Retired 1997
Secondary Market Value: $28

PILLOW PALS™ TOP FIVE

*T*his section showcases the five most valuable *Pillow Pals* as determined by their secondary market values. The secondary market is relatively quiet for this collection and many of the pieces listed here are early retired pieces or hard-to-find variations of the original version.

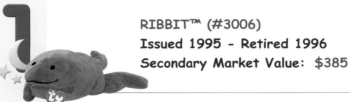

RIBBIT™ (#3006)
Issued 1995 - Retired 1996
Secondary Market Value: $385

SNAP™ (#3007)
Issued 1995 - Retired 1996
Secondary Market Value: $375

MEOW™ (#3011)
Gray Version
Issued 1997 - Retired 1998
Secondary Market Value: $130

ZULU™ (#3014)
Thin Stripes Version
Issued 1997 - Retired 1998
Secondary Market Value: $70

HUGGY™ (#3002)
SNUGGY™ (#3001)
Issued 1995 - Retired 1998
Secondary Market Value: $30

TY® PLUSH TOP FIVE

*T*his section showcases the five most valuable *Ty Plush* pieces as determined by their secondary market value. As the secondary market is relatively new to this collection, many prices have not yet been established. Therefore, some rare pieces, such as the early Himalayan cats, are not listed here, but are certainly very valuable!

PAPA SHAGGY™ (#9024)
Issued 1994 - Retired 1996
Secondary Market Value: $1,450

PAPA PUMPKIN™ (#9023)
Issued 1995 - Retired 1996
Secondary Market Value: $1,400

1991 TY COLLECTABLE BEAR™ (#5500)
Issued 1991 - Retired 1991
Secondary Market Value: $1,200

PAPA RUMPLES™ (#9022)
Issued 1995 - Retired 1996
Secondary Market Value: $1,000

MAX™ (#3001)
Issued 1988 - Retired 1990
Secondary Market Value: $910

HOW TO USE YOUR COLLECTOR'S VALUE GUIDE™

1. Locate your piece in the Value Guide. The guide is arranged by *Attic Treasures*, *Beanie Babies*, *Teenie Beanie Babies*, *Pillow Pals* and *Ty Plush*, which is broken down by bears, cats, dogs, country and wildlife. The pieces are listed alphabetically within their collection. To find a piece more quickly, refer to the *Index By Animal Type* or *Alphabetical Index* on pages 238 and 248, respectively. Note: Some items included are prototypes and may differ slightly from the actual piece. All sizes are approximate and may vary.

Abby™
8" • Bear • #6027
Issued: 1995 • Retired: 1998
A. Overalls w/Flower (1998)
B. Overalls (1996-97)
C. Ribbon (1995-96)
Market Value: ❹–$20 ❺–$25
❹–$65 ❺–$65 ❷–$135

2. Find the secondary market value of your piece. Some of the values are listed as "N/E," meaning the secondary market value for that particular piece has not been established. *Attic Treasures* and *Beanie Babies* secondary market values are determined by which generation tag is attached to the piece (for more details, see page 224) and the market value for each is listed next to the appropriate symbol. If a piece has a variation with a distinct secondary market value, the market value is listed next to the corresponding letter or description. For current pieces, fill in the current market price on the space provided (❼– $_____), which is usually the price you paid. All values listed are for animals in mint condition.

ATTIC TREASURES™

	Date Purchased	Tag Gen.	Price Paid	Value Of My Collection
1.	1/30	3	5.00	65.00
2.				
3.				
PENCIL TOTALS				

3. Record both the original price (what you actually paid), as well as the current value of the piece. Mark the prices in the corresponding boxes at the bottom of the page. Use a pencil so you can change the totals as your collection grows!

4. Calculate the total value for the entire page by adding together all of the boxes in each column. Don't forget to use pencil for this part as well.

5. Transfer the totals from each page to the *Total Value Of My Collection* worksheets. You can find this convenient chart located on pages 210-212.

6. Add all of the totals together to determine the overall value of your collection.

A TREASURY OF OLD FRIENDS

In January 1999, 17 new pieces made their way into *The Attic Treasures Collection*, including five pieces which were formerly in the *Ty Plush* category, bringing the total number in the collection to 119. In addition, the newly introduced pieces all sport a new swing tag, marking a 7th generation. All *Attic Treasures* pieces are valued according to their swing tag generation (see chart).

ATTIC TREASURES™ TAG KEY

 7– 7th Generation

 6– 6th Generation

 5– 5th Generation

 4– 4th Generation

 3– 3rd Generation

 2– 2nd Generation

 1– 1st Generation

1

Abby™
8" • Bear • #6027
Issued: 1995 • Retired: 1998
A. Overalls w/Flower (1998)
B. Overalls (1996-97)
C. Ribbon (1995-96)
**Market Value: 6–$20 5–$25
4–$65 3–$65 2–$135**

2

Amethyst™
13" • Cat • #6131
Issued: 1998 • Retired: 1998
Market Value: 6–$25

3 New!

Azalea™
8" • Bunny • #6093
Issued: 1999 • Current
Market Value: 7–$____

ATTIC TREASURES™

	Date Purchased	Tag Gen.	Price Paid	Value Of My Collection
1.				
2.				
3.				
PENCIL TOTALS				

(4)

Baby Curly™
(moved from Ty Plush in 1999)
12" • Bear • #5018
Issued: 1993 • Current
A. Sweater, Ty Plush Swing Tag (1998-Current)
B. Ribbon, Ty Plush Swing Tag (1993-98)
Market Value: A-$_____ B-N/E

(5)

Barry™
8" • Bear • #6073
Issued: 1997 • Retired: 1997
Market Value: ⑤-$112

(6)

Bearington™
14" • Bear • #6102
Issued: 1998 • Retired: 1998
Market Value: ⑥-$18

(7) *New!*

Beezee™
8" • Bumble Bee • #6088
Issued: 1999 • Current
Market Value: ⑦-$_____

ATTIC TREASURES™

	Date Purchased	Tag Gen.	Price Paid	Value Of My Collection
4.				
5.				
6.				
7.				
8.				
PENCIL TOTALS				

(8)

Benjamin™
9" • Rabbit • #6023
Issued: 1995 • Retired: 1997
A. Sweater (1996-97)
B. Ribbon (1995-96)
Market Value: ⑤-$55 ②-$122

9

Bloom™
16" • Rabbit • #6122
Issued: 1998 • Retired: 1998
Market Value: ⑥-$23

10

Bluebeary™
8" • Bear • #6080
Issued: 1998 • Current
Market Value: ⑦-$_____ ⑥-$12

11

Bonnie™
9" • Chick • #6075
Issued: 1998 • Current
Market Value: ⑦-$_____ ⑥-$11

12

Boris™
12" • Bear • #6041
Issued: 1996 • Retired: 1997
A. Vest (1996-97)
B. No Clothes (1996)
Market Value: ⑤-$48

13

Brewster™
9" • Dog • #6034
Issued: 1995 • Retired: 1997
A. Overalls (1996-97)
B. No Clothes (1995-96)
Market Value: ⑤-$32 ④-$45 ③-$55
②-$60 (Overalls), $70 (No Clothes)

ATTIC TREASURES™

	Date Purchased	Tag Gen.	Price Paid	Value Of My Collection
9.				
10.				
11.				
12.				
13.				
PENCIL TOTALS				

14

New!

Bugsy™
8" • Ladybug • #6089
Issued: 1999 • Current
Market Value: ⑦-$_____

15

New!

Camelia™
8" • Bunny • #6094
Issued: 1999 • Current
Market Value: ⑦-$_____

16

Carlton™
16" • Bear • #6064
Issued: 1996 • Retired: 1997
A. Overalls (1996-97)
B. Ribbon (1996)
Market Value: ⑤-$43

17

Casanova™
8" • Bear • #6073
Issued: 1998 • Retired: 1999
Market Value: ⑦-$9 ⑥-$12

ATTIC TREASURES™

	Date Purchased	Tag Gen.	Price Paid	Value Of My Collection
14.				
15.				
16.				
17.				
18.				
PENCIL TOTALS				

18

Cassie™
12" • Bear • #6028
Issued: 1995 • Retired: 1997
A. Bloomers (1996-97)
B. Ribbon (1995-96)
Market Value: ⑤-$95 ④-$150 (Bloomers),
$175 (Ribbon) ③-$180 ②-$235

ATTIC TREASURES™

(19) *New!*

Cawley™
10" • Crow • #6090
Issued: 1999 • Current
Market Value: ⑦-$_____

(20)

Charles™
12" • Bear • #6039
Issued: 1996 • Retired: 1997
A. Overalls (1996-97)
B. No Clothes (1996)
Market Value: ⑤-$43

(21)

Checkers™
8" • Panda • #6031
Issued: 1995 • Current
A. No Clothes (1998-Current)
B. Vest (1996-97)
C. No Clothes (1995-96)
Market Value: ⑦-$_____ ⑥-$14
⑤-$25 ④-$52 ③-$72 ②-$105

(22)

Chelsea™
8" • Bear • #6070
Issued: 1996 • Retired: 1998
Market Value: ⑥-$16 ⑤-$20

(23)

Christopher™
8" • Bear • #6071
Issued: 1996 • Retired: 1998
Market Value: ⑥-$17 ⑤-$22

ATTIC TREASURES™

	Date Purchased	Tag Gen.	Price Paid	Value Of My Collection
19.				
20.				
21.				
22.				
23.				
PENCIL TOTALS				

43

(24)

Clifford™
12" • Bear • #6003
Issued: 1993 • Retired: 1995
A. Green Ribbon (1994-95)
B. Red Ribbon (1993)
Market Value: ❶-$380

(25)

Clyde™
12" • Bear • #6040
Issued: 1996 • Retired: 1997
A. Vest (1996-97)
B. No Clothes (1996)
Market Value: ❺-$42

(26)

Cody™
8" • Bear • #6030
Issued: 1995 • Current
Market Value: ❼-$_____   ❻-$13
❺-$15   ❹-$43   ❸-$54   ❷-$85

(27)

Colby™
11" • Mouse • #6043
Issued: 1996 • Retired: 1997
A. Bloomers (1996-97)
B. No Clothes (1996)
Market Value: ❺-$75

ATTIC TREASURES™

	Date Purchased	Tag Gen.	Price Paid	Value Of My Collection
24.				
25.				
26.				
27.				
28.				
PENCIL TOTALS				

(28)

Copperfield™
16" • Bear • #6060
Issued: 1996 • Retired: 1997
A. Sweater (1996-97)
B. Ribbon (1996)
Market Value: ❺-$64

29

Curly™
(moved from Ty Plush in 1999)
18" • Bear • #5302
Issued: 1991 • Current
A. 18", Sweater, Ty Plush Swing Tag
(1998-Current)
B. 18", Ribbon, Ty Plush Swing Tag (1993-98)
C. 22", Ty Plush Swing Tag (1991-92)
Market Value: A–$_____ B/C–N/E

30

Curly Bunny™
(moved from Ty Plush in 1999)
22" • Bunny • #8017
Issued: 1992 • Current
A. Sweater, Ty Plush Swing Tag (1998-Current)
B. No Clothes, Ty Plush Swing Tag (1992-98)
Market Value: A–$_____ B–N/E

31

Curly Bunny™
(moved from Ty Plush in 1999)
22" • Bunny • #8018
Issued: 1992 • Current
A. Sweater, Ty Plush Swing Tag (1998-Current)
B. No Clothes, Ty Plush Swing Tag (1992-1998)
Market Value: A–$_____ B–N/E

32

Dexter™
9" • Bear • #6009
Issued: 1993 • Retired: 1997
A. Overalls (1996-97)
B. Ribbon (1993-96)
**Market Value: ⑤–$24 ④–$64
③–$70 ②–$100 ①–$120**

33

Dickens™
8" • Bear • #6038
Issued: 1996 • Retired: 1998
A. No Clothes (1998)
B. Overalls (1996-97)
C. No Clothes (1996)
Market Value: ⑥–$18 ⑤–$22 ④–$57

Attic Treasures™

	Date Purchased	Tag Gen.	Price Paid	Value Of My Collection
29.				
30.				
31.				
32.				
33.				
PENCIL TOTALS				

(34)

Digby™
12" • Bear • #6013
Issued: 1994 • Retired: 1997
A. Vest (1996-97)
B. Ribbon (1994-96)
Market Value: ❺-$70 ❹-$90
❸-N/E ❷-N/E ❶-$260

(35)

Domino™
12" • Panda • #6042
Issued: 1996 • Retired: 1997
A. Overalls (1996-97)
B. No Clothes (1996)
Market Value: ❺-$46

(36)

Ebony™
15" • Cat • #6063
Issued: 1996 • Retired: 1997
A. Bloomers (1996-97)
B. Ribbon (1996)
Market Value: ❺-$43

(37)

Ebony™
13" • Cat • #6130
Issued: 1998 • Retired: 1998
Market Value: ❻-$23

ATTIC TREASURES™

	Date Purchased	Tag Gen.	Price Paid	Value Of My Collection
34.				
35.				
36.				
37.				
38.				
PENCIL TOTALS				

(38)

Emily™
12" • Bear • #6016
Issued: 1994 • Retired: 1997
A. Dress/Hat (1996-97)
B. Bow (1995-96)
C. Ribbon/Small Feet (1994-95)
D. Ribbon/Big Feet (1994)
Market Value: ❺-$60 ❹-$90
❸-$160 ❷-$130 ❶-$160 (Bow), $130
(Ribbon/Small Feet), $210 (Ribbon/Big Feet)

ATTIC TREASURES™

(39)

Esmerelda™
8" • Bear • #6086
Issued: 1998 • Retired: 1998
Market Value: ⑦–$18 ⑥–$24

(40)

Eve™
12" • Bear • #6106
Issued: 1998 • Current
Market Value: ⑦–$_____ ⑥–$12

(41)

Fraser™
8" • Bear • #6010
Issued: 1993 • Retired: 1998
A. Sweater (1996-98)
B. Ribbon (1993-96)
Market Value: ⑥–$17
⑤–$17 (Sweater), $26 (Ribbon) ④–$56
③–$72 ②–$125 ①–$300

(42)

Frederick™
8" • Bear • #6072
Issued: 1996 • Retired: 1997
Market Value: ⑤–$48

(43)

Gem™
13" • Bear • #6107
Issued: 1998 • Retired: 1998
Market Value: ⑦–$14

ATTIC TREASURES™

	Date Purchased	Tag Gen.	Price Paid	Value Of My Collection
39.				
40.				
41.				
42.				
43.				
PENCIL TOTALS				

44
New!

Georgette™
9" • Goose • #6091
Issued: 1999 • Current
Market Value: ❼–$_____

45
New!

Georgia™
8" • Bunny • #6095
Issued: 1999 • Current
Market Value: ❼–$_____

46

Gilbert™
8" • Bear • #6006
Issued: 1993 • Retired: 1997
A. Overalls (1996-97)
B. Ribbon (1993-96)
Market Value: ❺–$28 ❶–$210

47

Gilbert™
8" • Bear • #6015
Issued: 1993 • Retired: 1993
Market Value: ❶–$370

ATTIC TREASURES™

	Date Purchased	Tag Gen.	Price Paid	Value Of My Collection
44.				
45.				
46.				
47.				
48.				
PENCIL TOTALS				

48

Gloria™
12" • Rabbit • #6123
Issued: 1998 • Retired: 1998
Market Value: ❻–$58

ATTIC TREASURES™

(49) New!

Gordon™
13" • Bear • #6110
Issued: 1999 • Current
Market Value: ⑦-$_____

(50)

Grace™
12" • Hippopotamus • #6142
Issued: 1998 • Retired: 1998
Market Value: ⑥-$18

(51)

Grady™
16" • Bear • #6051
Issued: 1996 • Retired: 1997
A. Vest (1996-97)
B. Ribbon (1996)
Market Value: ⑤-$75

(52)

Grant™
13" • Bear • #6101
Issued: 1998 • Current
Market Value: ⑦-$_____ ⑥-$14

(53)

Grover™
16" • Bear • #6050
Issued: 1995 • Retired: 1997
A. Overalls (1996-97)
B. Ribbon (1995-96)
Market Value: ⑤-$35 ④-$65
③-$75 ②-$92

ATTIC TREASURES™

	Date Purchased	Tag Gen.	Price Paid	Value Of My Collection
49.				
50.				
51.				
52.				
53.				
PENCIL TOTALS				

54

Grover™
13" • Bear • #6100
Issued: 1998 • Retired: 1998
Market Value: ⑥-$25

55

Grover Gold™
16" • Bear • #6051
Issued: 1995 • Retired: 1997
A. Vest (Est. 1997)
B. Ribbon (Est. 1995)
Market Value: ⑤-$50 ④-$57

56

New!

Heartley™
12" • Bear • #6111
Issued: 1999 • Current
Market Value: ⑦-$____

57

Heather™
20" • Rabbit • #6061
Issued: 1996 • Retired: 1997
A. Overalls (1996-97)
B. Ribbon (1996)
Market Value: ⑥-$42

ATTIC TREASURES™

	Date Purchased	Tag Gen.	Price Paid	Value Of My Collection
54.				
55.				
56.				
57.				
58.				
PENCIL TOTALS				

58

Henry™
8" • Bear • #6005
Issued: 1993 • Retired: 1997
A. Overalls (1996-97)
B. Green Ribbon/Brown (1994-96)
C. Blue Ribbon/Gold (1993)
D. Red Ribbon/Gold (1993)
Market Value: ⑥-$32
**①-$210 (Green Ribbon/Brown), $1,100
(Blue Ribbon/Gold), N/E (Red Ribbon/Gold)**

(59)

Iris™
10" • Rabbit • #6077
Issued: 1998 • Retired: 1998
Market Value: ⑦–$11 ⑥–$13

(60)

Isabella™
13" • Bear • #6109
Issued: 1998 • Current
Market Value: ⑦–$____

(61)

Ivan™
8" • Bear • #6029
Issued: 1995 • Current
Market Value: ⑦–$____ ⑥–$12
⑤–$20 ④–$65 ③–$70 ②–$120

(62)

Ivory™
15" • Cat • #6062
Issued: 1996 • Retired: 1997
A. Overalls (1996-97)
B. Ribbon (1996)
Market Value: ⑤–$60

(63)

Ivy™
10" • Rabbit • #6076
Issued: 1998 • Retired: 1998
Market Value: ⑦–$11 ⑥–$13

ATTIC TREASURES™

	Date Purchased	Tag Gen.	Price Paid	Value Of My Collection
59.				
60.				
61.				
62.				
63.				
PENCIL TOTALS				

(64)

Jack™
(exclusive to U.K.)
13" • Bear • #6989
Issued: 1998 • Current
Market Value: ❼–$_____ ❻–N/E

(65)

Jangle™
8" • Bear • #6082
Issued: 1998 • Retired: 1998
Market Value: ❼–$17

(66)

Jeremy™
12" • Hare • #6008
Issued: 1993 • Retired: 1997
A. Overalls (1997)
B. Vest (1996-97)
C. Ribbon (1993-96)
**Market Value: ❺–$44 ❹–$85
❸–$85 ❷–$130 ❶–$280**

(67)

Justin™
14" • Monkey • #6044
Issued: 1996 • Retired: 1997
A. Sweater (1996-97)
B. No Clothes (1996)
Market Value: ❺–$58

ATTIC TREASURES™

	Date Purchased	Tag Gen.	Price Paid	Value Of My Collection
64.				
65.				
66.				
67.				
PENCIL TOTALS				

ATTIC TREASURES™

68

King™
9" • Frog • #6049
Issued: 1996 • Retired: 1997
A. Cape (1996-97)
B. No Clothes (1996)
Market Value: ⑤-$47

69

King™
11" • Frog • #6140
Issued: 1998 • Retired: 1998
Market Value: ⑥-$32

70

Large Curly™
(moved from Ty Plush in 1999)
26" • Bear • #9019
Issued: 1992 • Current
A. Sweater, Ty Plush Swing Tag (1998-Current)
B. Ribbon, Ty Plush Swing Tag (1992-98)
Market Value: A-$_____ B-N/E

71

Laurel™
8" • Bear • #6081
Issued: 1998 • Retired: 1998
Market Value: ⑦-$18

72

Lilly™
9" • Lamb • #6037
Issued: 1995 • Retired: 1998
A. Bloomers (1996-98)
B. Ribbon (1995-96)
**Market Value: ⑥-$23 ⑤-$30
④-$105 ③-$110 ②-$160**

ATTIC TREASURES™

	Date Purchased	Tag Gen.	Price Paid	Value Of My Collection
68.				
69.				
70.				
71.				
72.				
PENCIL TOTALS				

(73)

PHOTO UNAVAILABLE

Mackenzie™
(exclusive to Canada)
13" • Bear • #6999
Issued: 1998 • Current
Market Value: ❼–$_____ ❻–N/E

(74)

Madison™
10" • Cow • #6035
Issued: 1995 • Retired: 1998
A. Overalls (1996-98)
B. Ribbon (1995-96)
Market Value: ❻–$25 ❺–$30
❹–$79 ❸–$85 ❷–$155

(75)

Malcolm™
12" • Bear • #6026
Issued: 1995 • Retired: 1997
A. Sweater (1996-97)
B. Ribbon (1995-96)
Market Value: ❺–$50 ❹–$78
❸–$88 ❷–$140

(76)

Mason™
8" • Bear • #6020
Issued: 1995 • Retired: 1998
A. Sweater (1996-98)
B. Ribbon (1995-96)
Market Value: ❻–$22 ❺–$28
❹–$55 ❸–$90 ❷–$120

ATTIC TREASURES™

	Date Purchased	Tag Gen.	Price Paid	Value Of My Collection
73.				
74.				
75.				
76.				
77.				
PENCIL TOTALS				

(77)

Montgomery™
15" • Moose • #6143
Issued: 1998 • Retired: 1998
Market Value: ❻–$24

(78)

Morgan™
8" • Monkey • #6018
Issued: 1994 • Retired: 1998
A. Vest (1996-98)
B. No Clothes/Shaved Face (1996)
C. Ribbon/Furry Face (1994-95)
Market Value: ⑥–$17 ⑤–$24
②–N/E ①–$220

(79)

Murphy™
9" • Dog • #6033
Issued: 1995 • Retired: 1997
A. Overalls (1996-97)
B. No Clothes (1995-96)
Market Value: ⑤–$33 ④–$50
③–$65 ②–$80

(80)

Nicholas™
8" • Bear • #6015
Issued: 1994 • Retired: 1998
A. Sweater (1996-98)
B. Ribbon (1994-96)
Market Value: ⑥–$23 ⑤–$29 ④–$105
③–N/E ②–N/E ①–$320

(81)

Nola™
12" • Bear • #6014
Issued: 1994 • Retired: 1997
A. Dress/Hat (1996-97)
B. Bow/Small Feet (1995-96)
C. Ribbon/Big Feet (1994-95)
Market Value: ⑤–$85 ④–$100 ③–$125
②–$145 ①–$175 (Bow/Small Feet),
$220 (Ribbon/Big Feet)

(82)

Oscar™
8" • Bear • #6025
Issued: 1995 • Retired: 1998
A. Overalls (1996-98)
B. Ribbon (1995-96)
Market Value: ⑥–$21 ⑤–$30
④–$55 ③–$60 ②–$105

ATTIC TREASURES™

	Date Purchased	Tag Gen.	Price Paid	Value Of My Collection
78.				
79.				
80.				
81.				
82.				
PENCIL TOTALS				

(83)

Penelope™
9" • Pig • #6036
Issued: 1995 • Retired: 1997
A. Overalls (1996-97)
B. No Clothes (1995-96)
Market Value: ⑤-$55 ④-$85
③-$100 ②-$135

(84)

Peppermint™
8" • Polar Bear • #6074
Issued: 1998 • Current
Market Value: ⑦-$_____ ⑥-$12

(85)

Peter™
8" • Bear • #6084
Issued: 1998 • Retired: 1998
Market Value: ⑦-$18 ⑥-$24

(86)

Piccadilly™
9" • Bear • #6069
Issued: 1998 • Current
A. Multi-Color Striped Suit (1999)
B. Blue/Green Suit (1998)
Market Value: ⑦-$_____ ⑥-$16

ATTIC TREASURES™

	Date Purchased	Tag Gen.	Price Paid	Value Of My Collection
83.				
84.				
85.				
86.				
87.				
PENCIL TOTALS				

(87)

Pouncer™
8" • Cat • #6011
Issued: 1994 • Current
A. Bloomers (1998-Current)
B. Sweater (1996-97)
C. Ribbon/Gold & White (1995-96)
D. Ribbon/Gold (1994-95)
Market Value: ⑦-$_____ ⑥-$14
⑤-$22 ④-N/E ③-$225 ②-$225
①-N/E (Ribbon/Gold & White),
$325 (Ribbon/Gold)

88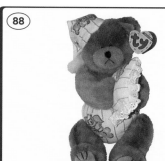

Precious™
12" • Bear • #6104
Issued: 1998 • Retired: 1998
Market Value: ⑥-$18

89

Prince™
7" • Frog • #6048
Issued: 1996 • Retired: 1998
Market Value: ⑥-$16 ⑤-$21

90

Priscilla™
12" • Pig • #6045
Issued: 1996 • Retired: 1997
A. Overalls (1996-97)
B. No Clothes (1996)
Market Value: ⑤-$50

91

Purrcy™
8" • Cat • #6022
Issued: 1995 • Current
A. Bloomers (1998-Current)
B. Overalls (1996-97)
C. Ribbon (1995-96)
Market Value: ⑦-$_____ ⑥-$14
⑤-$23 ④-$105 ③-$115 ②-$210

92 *New!*

Radcliffe™
9" • Raccoon • #6087
Issued: 1999 • Current
Market Value: ⑦-$_____

ATTIC TREASURES™

	Date Purchased	Tag Gen.	Price Paid	Value Of My Collection
88.				
89.				
90.				
91.				
92.				
PENCIL TOTALS				

(93) *New!*

Ramsey™
9" • Ram • #6092
Issued: 1999 • Current
Market Value: ⑦-$_____

(94)

Rebecca™
12" • Bear • #6019
Issued: 1995 • Retired: 1997
A. Overalls (1996-97)
B. Bow (1995-96)
Market Value: ⑤-$63 ④-$120
③-$145 ②-$295

(95)

Reggie™
8" • Bear • #6004
Issued: 1993 • Retired: 1995
A. Navy Ribbon (1994-95)
B. Green Ribbon (1994)
C. Red Ribbon (1993)
Market Value: ❶-$475 (Navy Ribbon),
N/E (Green Ribbon), $570 (Red Ribbon)

(96)

Rose™
10" • Rabbit • #6078
Issued: 1998 • Retired: 1998
Market Value: ⑦-13 ⑥-$15

ATTIC TREASURES™

	Date Purchased	Tag Gen.	Price Paid	Value Of My Collection
93.				
94.				
95.				
96.				
97.				
PENCIL TOTALS				

(97)

Samuel™
13" • Bear • #6105
Issued: 1998 • Current
Market Value: ⑦-$_____ ⑥-$13

58

ATTIC TREASURES™

(98)

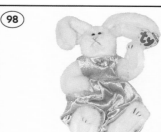

Sara™
12" • Hare • #6007
Issued: 1993 • Retired: 1997
A. Bloomers (1996-97)
B. Ribbon (1993-96)
Market Value: ❺–$52 ❹–$100
❸–$135 ❷–$195 ❶–$315

(99)

Sara™
15" • Rabbit • #6120
Issued: 1998 • Current
Market Value: ❼–$_____ ❻–$12

(100)

Scooter™
9" • Dog • #6032
Issued: 1995 • Retired: 1997
A. Vest (1996-97)
B. No Clothes (1995-96)
Market Value: ❺–$44 ❹–$65
❸–$70 ❷–$85

(101)

Scotch™
14" • Bear • #6103
Issued: 1998 • Retired: 1998
Market Value: ❻–$24

(102)

Scruffy™
9" • Dog • #6085
Issued: 1998 • Current
Market Value: ❼–$_____ ❻–$12

Attic Treasures™

	Date Purchased	Tag Gen.	Price Paid	Value Of My Collection
98.				
99.				
100.				
101.				
102.				
PENCIL TOTALS				

(103)

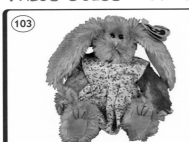

Shelby™
9" • Rabbit • #6024
Issued: 1995 • Retired: 1998
A. Dress (1996-98)
B. Ribbon (1995-96)
**Market Value: ⑥-$22 ⑤-$30
④-N/E ③-N/E ②-$160**

(104)

Sidney™
15" • Rabbit • #6121
Issued: 1998 • Retired: 1998
Market Value: ⑥-$23

(105)

Sire™
13" • Lion • #6141
Issued: 1998 • Retired: 1998
Market Value: ⑥-$22

(106)

New!

Skylar™
9" • Bear • #6096
Issued: 1999 • Retired: 1999
Market Value: ⑦-$14

ATTIC TREASURES™

	Date Purchased	Tag Gen.	Price Paid	Value Of My Collection
103.				
104.				
105.				
106.				
PENCIL TOTALS				

(107)

Spencer™
15" • Dog • #6046
Issued: 1996 • Retired: 1997
A. Sweater (1996-97)
B. No Clothes (1996)
Market Value: ❺–$47

(108)

Squeaky™
8" • Mouse • #6017
Issued: 1994 • Retired: 1998
A. No Clothes/Gray & White/Pink Nose &
White Whiskers (1995-98)
B. Ribbon/Gray/Black Nose & Whiskers (1994)
Market Value: ❻–$17 ❺–$21
❶–$225 (No Clothes), $200 (Ribbon)

(109)

Sterling™
8" • Bear • #6083
Issued: 1998 • Current
Market Value: ❼–$_____

(110)

Strawbunny™
10" • Rabbit • #6079
Issued: 1998 • Current
Market Value: ❼–$_____ ❻–$12

(111)

Tiny Tim™
8" • Bear • #6001
Issued: 1993 • Retired: 1997
A. Overalls (1996-97)
B. Ribbon (1993-96)
Market Value: ❺–$30 ❹–$56
❸–$72 ❷–$90 ❶–$140

ATTIC TREASURES™

	Date Purchased	Tag Gen.	Price Paid	Value Of My Collection
107.				
108.				
109.				
110.				
111.				
PENCIL TOTALS				

(112)

Tracy™
15" • Dog • #6047
Issued: 1996 • Retired: 1997
A. Overalls (1996-97)
B. No Clothes (1996)
Market Value: ⑤-$38

(113)

Tyler™
12" • Bear • #6002
Issued: 1993 • Retired: 1997
A. Sweater (1996-97)
B. Ribbon (1993-96)
**Market Value: ⑤-$43 ④-$75
③-$80 ②-$120 ①-$180**

(114)

Tyrone™
13" • Bear • #6108
Issued: 1998 • Current
Market Value: ⑦-$_____

(115)

Watson™
14" • Bear • #6065
Issued: 1996 • Retired: 1997
A. Overalls (1996-97)
B. Ribbon (1996)
Market Value: ⑤-$45

ATTIC TREASURES™

	Date Purchased	Tag Gen.	Price Paid	Value Of My Collection
112.				
113.				
114.				
115.				
116.				
PENCIL TOTALS				

(116)

Wee Willie™
8" • Bear • #6021
Issued: 1995 • Retired: 1997
A. Overalls (1996-97)
B. Ribbon (1995-96)
**Market Value: ⑤-$24 ④-$50
③-$60 ②-$105**

(117)

Whiskers™
8" • Cat • #6012
Issued: 1994 • Current
A. Bloomers (1998-Current)
B. Overalls (1996-97)
C. Ribbon/Gray & White (1995-96)
D. Ribbon/Gray (1994-95)
**Market Value: ⑦-$_____ ⑥-$14
⑤-$22 ❶-$330**

(118)

Woolie™
6" • Bear • #6011
Issued: 1993 • Retired: 1993
Market Value: ❶-$1,200

(119)

Woolie™
6" • Bear • #6012
(appears in 1993 Ty® catalog,
production not confirmed)
Issued: 1993 • Retired: 1993
Market Value: N/E

ATTIC TREASURES™

	Date Purchased	Tag Gen.	Price Paid	Value Of My Collection
117.				
118.				
119.				
PENCIL TOTALS				

Value Guide - Future Releases

Use this page to record future Attic Treasures™ releases.

Attic Treasures™	Date Purchased	Tag Gen.	Price Paid	Value Of My Collection
PENCIL TOTALS				

A BONANZA OF NEW BEANIE BABIES®

To help ring in the new year, 24 new *Beanie Babies* joined the family on January 1, 1999, bringing the total number of pieces in the collection to 190. On the other end of the spectrum, 16 old favorites were honored with retirement on March 31, 1999, bringing the number of retired pieces to 143, including three bears that were never available in retail stores. Pieces which have been available as promotional giveaways at sporting events are noted with their corresponding symbols in the upper right corner of their boxes. A complete listing of these promotions is included in the *Sports Promotion Beanie Babies®* section on pages 107-109.

The market value for each *Beanie Baby* is based on the generation of swing tag attached to the piece (see chart below and the *Swing Tags* section on page 224 for additional information).

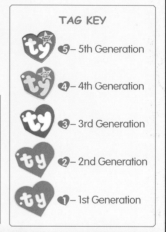

TAG KEY

5 – 5th Generation

4 – 4th Generation

3 – 3rd Generation

2 – 2nd Generation

1 – 1st Generation

SPORTS PROMOTION BEANIE BABIES® KEY

Canadian Special Olympics

National Basketball Association

National Hockey League

Major League Baseball

National Football League

Women's National Basketball Association

#1 Bear™
(exclusive Ty sales representative gift)
10" • Bear • N/A • Born: N/A
Issued: 12/98 • Not Avail. In Retail Stores
Market Value: Special Tag – **$10,000**

BEANIE BABIES®

	Date Purchased	Tag Gen.	Price Paid	Value Of My Collection
1.				
PENCIL TOTALS				

2

1997 Teddy™
10" • Bear • #4200 • Born: 12/25/96
Issued: 10/97 • Retired: 12/97
Market Value: ④–$55

3

1998 Holiday Teddy™
10" • Bear • #4204 • Born: 12/25/98
Issued: 9/98 • Retired: 12/98
Market Value: ⑤–$60

4

New!

1999 Signature Bear™
10" • Bear • #4228 • Born: N/A
Issued: 1/99 • Current
Market Value: ⑤–$_____

5

Ally™
12" • Alligator • #4032 • Born: 3/14/94
Issued: 6/94 • Retired: 10/97
Market Value: ④–$60 ③–$130
⑤–$270 ①–$400

Beanie Babies®

	Date Purchased	Tag Gen.	Price Paid	Value Of My Collection
2.				
3.				
4.				
5.				
6.				
PENCIL TOTALS				

6

Ants™
12" • Anteater • #4195 • Born: 11/7/97
Issued: 5/98 • Retired: 12/98
Market Value: ⑤–$13

BEANIE BABIES®

7

Baldy™
8" • Eagle • #4074 • Born: 2/17/96
Issued: 5/97 • Retired: 5/98
Market Value: ⑤–**$20** ④–**$24**

8

A

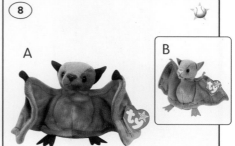

B

Batty™
5" • Bat • #4035 • Born: 10/29/96
Issued: 10/97 • Retired: 3/99
A. Tie-dye (10/98-3/99) ⑤–**$30**
B. Brown (10/97-10/98) ⑤–**$15** ④–**$21**

9

Beak™
7" • Kiwi • #4211 • Born: 2/3/98
Issued: 9/98 • Current
Market Value: ⑤–**$_____**

10

Bernie™
10" • St. Bernard • #4109 • Born: 10/3/96
Issued: 1/97 • Retired: 9/98
Market Value: ⑤–**$12** ④–**$16**

11

Bessie™
10" • Cow • #4009 • Born: 6/27/95
Issued: 6/95 • Retired: 10/97
Market Value: ④–**$70** ③–**$140**

BEANIE BABIES®

	Date Purchased	Tag Gen.	Price Paid	Value Of My Collection
7.				
8.				
9.				
10.				
11.				
PENCIL TOTALS				

67

12

Billionaire Bear™
(exclusive Ty employee gift)
10" • Bear • N/A • Born: N/A
Issued: 10/98 • Not Avail. In Retail Stores
Market Value: Special Tag –$3,800

13

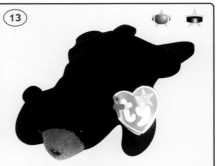

Blackie™
10" • Bear • #4011 • Born: 7/15/94
Issued: 6/94 • Retired: 9/98
Market Value: ⑤–$17 ④–$20
③–$110 ②–$250 ①–$360

14

Blizzard™
10" • Tiger • #4163 • Born: 12/12/96
Issued: 5/97 • Retired: 5/98
Market Value: ⑤–$22 ④–$26

15

Bones™
10" • Dog • #4001 • Born: 1/18/94
Issued: 6/94 • Retired: 5/98
Market Value: ⑤–$22 ④–$26
③–$115 ②–$250 ①–$330

BEANIE BABIES®

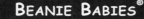

	Date Purchased	Tag Gen.	Price Paid	Value Of My Collection
12.				
13.				
14.				
15.				
16.				
PENCIL TOTALS				

16

A

B

Bongo™
(name changed from "Nana™")
9" • Monkey • #4067 • Born: 8/17/95
Issued: 6/95 • Retired: 12/98
Market Value:
A. Tan Tail (6/95-12/98)
⑤–$13 ④–$17 ③–$150
B. Brown Tail (2/96-6/96) ④–$70 ③–$150

(17)

Britannia™
(exclusive to Great Britain)
10" • Bear • #4601 • Born: 12/15/97
Issued: 12/97 • Current
Market Value (in U.S. market): 5–$385

(18)

Bronty™
7" • Brontosaurus • #4085 • Born: N/A
Issued: 6/95 • Retired: 6/96
Market Value: 3–$1,075

(19)

Brownie™
(name changed to "Cubbie™")
10" • Bear • #4010 • Born: N/A
Issued: 1/94 • Retired: 1994
Market Value: 1–$4,100

(20)

Bruno™
10" • Dog • #4183 • Born: 9/9/97
Issued: 12/97 • Retired: 9/98
Market Value: 5–$13

(21)

Bubbles™
8" • Fish • #4078 • Born: 7/2/95
Issued: 6/95 • Retired: 5/97
Market Value: 4–$160 3–$220

BEANIE BABIES®

	Date Purchased	Tag Gen.	Price Paid	Value Of My Collection
17.				
18.				
19.				
20.				
21.				
PENCIL TOTALS				

BEANIE BABIES®

22

Bucky™
11" • Beaver • #4016 • Born: 6/8/95
Issued: 1/96 • Retired: 12/97
Market Value: *4*–**$40** *3*–**$120**

23

Bumble™
6" • Bee • #4045 • Born: 10/16/95
Issued: 6/95 • Retired: 6/96
Market Value: *4*–**$645** *3*–**$600**

24

New!

Butch™
10" • Bull Terrier • #4227 • Born: 10/2/98
Issued: 1/99 • Current
Market Value: *5*–**$_____**

25

Canyon™
9" • Cougar • #4212 • Born: 5/29/98
Issued: 9/98 • Current
Market Value: *5*–**$_____**

Beanie Babies®

	Date Purchased	Tag Gen.	Price Paid	Value Of My Collection
22.				
23.				
24.				
25.				
26.				
PENCIL TOTALS				

26

Caw™
10" • Crow • #4071 • Born: N/A
Issued: 6/95 • Retired: 6/96
Market Value: *3*–**$720**

27

Chilly™
10" • Polar Bear • #4012 • Born: N/A
Issued: 6/94 • Retired: 1/96
Market Value: ③–$2,000
②–$2,100 ①–$2,300

28

Chip™
10" • Cat • #4121 • Born: 1/26/96
Issued: 5/97 • Retired: 3/99
Market Value: ⑤–$10 ④–$16

29

Chocolate™
10" • Moose • #4015 • Born: 4/27/93
Issued: 1/94 • Retired: 12/98
Market Value: ⑤–$13 ④–$16
③–$140 ②–$300 ①–$475

30

Chops™
8" • Lamb • #4019 • Born: 5/3/96
Issued: 1/96 • Retired: 1/97
Market Value: ④–$185 ③–$250

31

Claude™
10" • Crab • #4083 • Born: 9/3/96
Issued: 5/97 • Retired: 12/98
Market Value: ⑤–$14 ④–$18

BEANIE BABIES®

	Date Purchased	Tag Gen.	Price Paid	Value Of My Collection
27.				
28.				
29.				
30.				
31.				
PENCIL TOTALS				

BEANIE BABIES®

(32)

Clubby™
**(exclusive to Beanie Babies®
Official Club™ members)**
10" • Bear • N/A • Born: 7/7/98
Issued: 5/98 • Retired: 3/99
Market Value: ⑤-$55

(33)

Congo™
8" • Gorilla • #4160 • Born: 11/9/96
Issued: 6/96 • Retired: 12/98
Market Value: ⑤-$13 ④-$16

(34)

Coral™
8" • Fish • #4079 • Born: 3/2/95
Issued: 6/95 • Retired: 1/97
Market Value: ④-$200 ③-$265

(35)

Crunch™
8" • Shark • #4130 • Born: 1/13/96
Issued: 1/97 • Retired: 9/98
Market Value: ⑤-$12 ④-$15

BEANIE BABIES®

	Date Purchased	Tag Gen.	Price Paid	Value Of My Collection
32.				
33.				
34.				
35.				
36.				
PENCIL TOTALS				

(36)

Cubbie™
(name changed from "Brownie™")
10" • Bear • #4010 • Born: 11/14/93
Issued: 1/94 • Retired: 12/97
**Market Value: ⑤-$32 ④-$32
③-$150 ②-$325 ①-$475**

(37)

Curly™
10" • Bear • #4052 • Born: 4/12/96
Issued: 6/96 • Retired: 12/98
Market Value: ⑤–**$28** ④–**$34**

(38)

Daisy™
10" • Cow • #4006 • Born: 5/10/94
Issued: 6/94 • Retired: 9/98
Market Value: ⑤–**$15** ④–**$20**
③–**$120** ②–**$240** ①–**$350**

(39)

B

A

Derby™
10" • Horse • #4008 • Born: 9/16/95
Issued: 6/95 • Current
Market Value:
A. Star/Fluffy Mane (1/99-Current)
⑤–**$**____
B. Star/Coarse Mane (12/97-1/99)
⑤–**$22**
C. Coarse Mane (Est. Late 95-12/97)
④–**$32** ③–**$575**
D. Fine Mane (Est. 6/95-Late 95)
③–**$3,500**

C

D

(40)

A

B

Digger™
10" • Crab • #4027 • Born: 8/23/95
Issued: 6/94 • Retired: 5/97
Market Value:
A. Red (6/95-5/97) ④–**$120** ③–**$260**
B. Orange (6/94-6/95) ③–**$750**
②–**$840** ①–**$925**

(41)

Doby™
10" • Doberman • #4110 • Born: 10/9/96
Issued: 1/97 • Retired: 12/98
Market Value: ⑤–**$13** ④–**$15**

BEANIE BABIES®

	Date Purchased	Tag Gen.	Price Paid	Value Of My Collection
37.				
38.				
39.				
40.				
41.				
PENCIL TOTALS				

BEANIE BABIES®

73

(42)

Doodle™
(name changed to "Strut™")
8" • Rooster • #4171 • Born: 3/8/96
Issued: 5/97 • Retired: 1997
Market Value: ④–$48

(43)

Dotty™
10" • Dalmatian • #4100 • Born: 10/17/96
Issued: 5/97 • Retired: 12/98
Market Value: ⑤–$14 ④–$17

(44)

Early™
8" • Robin • #4190 • Born: 2/20/97 or 3/20/97
Issued: 5/98 • Current
Market Value: ⑤–$_____

(45)

Ears™
9" • Rabbit • #4018 • Born: 4/18/95
Issued: 1/96 • Retired: 5/98
Market Value: ⑤–$18 ④–$22 ③–$110

Beanie Babies®

	Date Purchased	Tag Gen.	Price Paid	Value Of My Collection
42.				
43.				
44.				
45.				
46.				
PENCIL TOTALS				

(46)

Echo™
10" • Dolphin • #4180 • Born: 12/21/96
Issued: 5/97 • Retired: 5/98
Market Value: ⑤–$20 ④–$24

(47) *New!*

Eggbert™
8" • Chick • #4232 • Born: 4/10/98
Issued: 1/99 • Current
Market Value: ⑤-$_____

(48)

Erin™
10" • Bear • #4186 • Born: 3/17/97
Issued: 1/98 • Current
Market Value: ⑤-$_____

(49) *New!*

Ewey™
9" • Lamb • #4219 • Born: 3/1/98
Issued: 1/99 • Current
Market Value: ⑤-$_____

(50)

Fetch™
9" • Golden Retriever • #4189 • Born: 2/4/97
Issued: 5/98 • Retired: 12/98
Market Value: ⑤-$18

(51)

Flash™
10" • Dolphin • #4021 • Born: 5/13/93
Issued: 1/94 • Retired: 5/97
Market Value: ④-$115 ③-$195
②-$330 ①-$450

BEANIE BABIES®

	Date Purchased	Tag Gen.	Price Paid	Value Of My Collection
47.				
48.				
49.				
50.				
51.				
PENCIL TOTALS				

(52)

Fleece™
9" • Lamb • #4125 • Born: 3/21/96
Issued: 1/97 • Retired: 12/98
Market Value: ⑤-$13 ④-$15

(53)

Flip™
10" • Cat • #4012 • Born: 2/28/95
Issued: 1/96 • Retired: 10/97
Market Value: ④-$38 ③-$125

(54)

Floppity™
10" • Bunny • #4118 • Born: 5/28/96
Issued: 1/97 • Retired: 5/98
Market Value: ⑤-$20 ④-$25

(55)

Flutter™
6" • Butterfly • #4043 • Born: N/A
Issued: 6/95 • Retired: 6/96
Market Value: ③-$1,075

BEANIE BABIES®

	Date Purchased	Tag Gen.	Price Paid	Value Of My Collection
52.				
53.				
54.				
55.				
56.				
PENCIL TOTALS				

(56)

Fortune™
10" • Panda • #4196 • Born: 12/6/97
Issued: 5/98 • Current
Market Value: ⑤-$_____

57

Freckles™
10" • Leopard • #4066 • Born: 6/3/96 or 7/28/96
Issued: 6/96 • Retired: 12/98
Market Value: ⑤–$13 ④–$16

58

New!

Fuzz™
10" • Bear • #4237 • Born: 7/23/98
Issued: 1/99 • Current
Market Value: ⑤–$_____

59

Garcia™
10" • Bear • #4051 • Born: 8/1/95
Issued: 1/96 • Retired: 5/97
Market Value: ④–$200 ③–$275

60

New!

Germania™
(exclusive to Germany)
10" • Bear • #4236 • Geburtstag: 10/3/98
Issued: 1/99 • Current
Market Value (in U.S. market): ⑤–$400

BEANIE BABIES®

	Date Purchased	Tag Gen.	Price Paid	Value Of My Collection
57.				
58.				
59.				
60.				
PENCIL TOTALS				

61

Gigi™
8" • Poodle • #4191 • Born: 4/7/97
Issued: 5/98 • Current
Market Value: ⑤–$_____

62

Glory™
10" • Bear • #4188 • Born: 7/4/97
Issued: 5/98 • Retired: 12/98
Market Value: ⑤–$40

63

New!

Goatee™
8" • Goat • #4235 • Born: 11/4/98
Issued: 1/99 • Current
Market Value: ⑤–$_____

64

Gobbles™
8" • Turkey • #4034 • Born: 11/27/96
Issued: 10/97 • Retired: 3/99
Market Value: ⑤–$12 ④–$20

BEANIE BABIES®

	Date Purchased	Tag Gen.	Price Paid	Value Of My Collection
61.				
62.				
63.				
64.				
65.				
PENCIL TOTALS				

65

Goldie™
8" • Goldfish • #4023 • Born: 11/14/94
Issued: 6/94 • Retired: 12/97
Market Value: ⑤–$45 ④–$45
③–$120 ②–$240 ①–$390

(66)
New!

Goochy™
10" • Jellyfish • #4230 • Born: 11/18/98
Issued: 1/99 • Current
Market Value: ⑤-$_____

(67)

Gracie™
8" • Swan • #4126 • Born: 6/17/96
Issued: 1/97 • Retired: 5/98
Market Value: ⑤-$18 ④-$21

(68)

Grunt™
10" • Razorback • #4092 • Born: 7/19/95
Issued: 1/96 • Retired: 5/97
Market Value: ④-$170 ③-$240

(69)

Halo™
10" • Angel • #4208 • Born: 8/31/98
Issued: 9/98 • Current
Market Value: ⑤-$_____

(70)   A

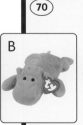
B

Happy™
10" • Hippo • #4061 • Born: 2/25/94
Issued: 6/94 • Retired: 5/98
Market Value:
A. Lavender (6/95-5/98)
⑤-$25 ④-$30 ③-$240
B. Gray (6/94-6/95)
③-$650 ②-$750 ①-$840

BEANIE BABIES®

	Date Purchased	Tag Gen.	Price Paid	Value Of My Collection
66.				
67.				
68.				
69.				
70.				
PENCIL TOTALS				

71 New!

Hippie™
10" • Bunny • #4218 • Born: 5/4/98
Issued: 1/99 • Current
Market Value: ⑤–$_____

72

Hippity™
10" • Bunny • #4119 • Born: 6/1/96
Issued: 1/97 • Retired: 5/98
Market Value: ⑤–$22 ④–$26

73

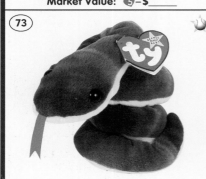

Hissy™
25" • Snake • #4185 • Born: 4/4/97
Issued: 12/97 • Retired: 3/99
Market Value: ⑤–$10

74

Hoot™
6" • Owl • #4073 • Born: 8/9/95
Issued: 1/96 • Retired: 10/97
Market Value: ④–$45 ③–$115

BEANIE BABIES®

	Date Purchased	Tag Gen.	Price Paid	Value Of My Collection
71.				
72.				
73.				
74.				
75.				
PENCIL TOTALS				

75 New!

Hope™
9" • Bear • #4213 • Born: 3/23/98
Issued: 1/99 • Current
Market Value: ⑤–$_____

(76)

Hoppity™
10" • Bunny • #4117 • Born: 4/3/96
Issued: 1/97 • Retired: 5/98
Market Value: ⑤–**$20** ④–**$25**

(77)

Humphrey™
10" • Camel • #4060 • Born: N/A
Issued: 6/94 • Retired: 6/95
Market Value: ③–**$2,100**
②–**$2,200** ①–**$2,400**

(78)

A

B

C

Iggy™
10" • Iguana • #4038 • Born: 8/12/97
Issued: 12/97 • Retired: 3/99
Market Value:
A. Blue/No Tongue (Mid 98-3/99)
⑤–**$14**
B. Tie-dye/With Tongue (6/98-Mid 98)
⑤–**$18**
C. Tie-dye/No Tongue (12/97-6/98)
⑤–**$23**

(79)

A

B

Inch™
12" • Inchworm • #4044 • Born: 9/3/95
Issued: 6/95 • Retired: 5/98
Market Value:
A. Yarn Antennas (Est. Mid 96-5/98)
⑤–**$25** ④–**$28**
B. Felt Antennas (Est. 6/95-Mid 96)
④–**$160** ③–**$175**

(80)

A

B

C

Inky™
8" • Octopus • #4028 • Born: 11/29/94
Issued: 6/94 • Retired: 5/98
Market Value:
A. Pink (6/95-5/98)
⑤–**$33** ④–**$38** ③–**$230**
B. Tan With Mouth (9/94-6/95)
③–**$630** ②–**$675**
C. Tan Without Mouth (6/94-9/94)
②–**$760** ①–**$825**

BEANIE BABIES®

	Date Purchased	Tag Gen.	Price Paid	Value Of My Collection
76.				
77.				
78.				
79.				
80.				
PENCIL TOTALS				

(81)

Jabber™
10" • Parrot • #4197 • Born: 10/10/97
Issued: 5/98 • Current
Market Value: ⑤–$_____

(82)

Jake™
9" • Mallard Duck • #4199 • Born: 4/16/97
Issued: 5/98 • Current
Market Value: ⑤–$_____

(83)

Jolly™
10" • Walrus • #4082 • Born: 12/2/96
Issued: 5/97 • Retired: 5/98
Market Value: ⑤–$20 ④–$23

(84)

New!

Kicks™
10" • Bear • #4229 • Born: 8/16/98
Issued: 1/99 • Current
Market Value: ⑤–$_____

BEANIE BABIES®

	Date Purchased	Tag Gen.	Price Paid	Value Of My Collection
81.				
82.				
83.				
84.				
85.				
PENCIL TOTALS				

(85)

Kiwi™
10" • Toucan • #4070 • Born: 9/16/95
Issued: 6/95 • Retired: 1/97
Market Value: ④–$175 ③–$250

86

Kuku™
10" • Cockatoo • #4192 • Born: 1/5/97
Issued: 5/98 • Current
Market Value: ⑤–$_____

87

Lefty™
8" • Donkey • #4085 • Born: 7/4/96
Issued: 6/96 • Retired: 1/97
Market Value: ④–$275

88

Legs™
10" • Frog • #4020 • Born: 4/25/93
Issued: 1/94 • Retired: 10/97
Market Value: ④–$25   ③–$100
②–$295   ①–$420

89

Libearty™
10" • Bear • #4057 • Born: Summer 1996
Issued: 6/96 • Retired: 1/97
Market Value: ④–$350

90

A

B

Lizzy™
12" • Lizard • #4033 • Born: 5/11/95
Issued: 6/95 • Retired: 12/97
Market Value:
A. Blue (1/96-12/97)
⑤–$30   ④–$30   ③–$295
B. Tie-dye (6/95-1/96)   ③–$1,025

BEANIE BABIES®

	Date Purchased	Tag Gen.	Price Paid	Value Of My Collection
86.				
87.				
88.				
89.				
90.				
PENCIL TOTALS				

91

Loosy™
8" • Goose • #4206 • Born: 3/29/98
Issued: 9/98 • Current
Market Value: ⑤-$_____

92

A

Lucky™
6" • Ladybug • #4040 • Born: 5/1/95
Issued: 6/94 • Retired: 5/98
Market Value:
A. Approx. 11 Printed Spots
(2/96-5/98) ⑤-**$25** ④-**$28**
B. Approx. 21 Printed Spots
(Est. Mid 96-Late 96) ④-**$500**
C. Approx. 7 Felt Glued-On Spots
(6/94-2/96) ③-**$205**
②-**$360** ①-**$450**

B

C

93 New!

Luke™
10" • Black Lab • #4214 • Born: 6/15/98
Issued: 1/99 • Current
Market Value: ⑤-$_____

94 New!

Mac™
9" • Cardinal • #4225 • Born: 6/10/98
Issued: 1/99 • Current
Market Value: ⑤-$_____

BEANIE BABIES®

	Date Purchased	Tag Gen.	Price Paid	Value Of My Collection
91.				
92.				
93.				
94.				
95.				
PENCIL TOTALS				

95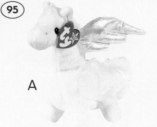

A

B

Magic™
10" • Dragon • #4088 • Born: 9/5/95
Issued: 6/95 • Retired: 12/97
Market Value:
A. Pale Pink Thread (6/95-12/97)
④-**$50** ③-**$130**
B. Hot Pink Thread (Est. Mid 96-Early 97) ④-**$70**

96

Manny™
9" • Manatee • #4081 • Born: 6/8/95
Issued: 1/96 • Retired: 5/97
Market Value: ④–**$165** ③–**$230**

97

A 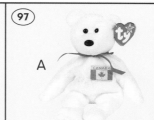 B

Maple™
(exclusive to Canada)
10" • Bear • #4600 • Born: 7/1/96
Issued: 1/97 • Current
Market Value (in U.S. market):
A. "Maple™" Tush Tag (Est. Early 97-Current)
⑤–**$210** ④–**$230**
B. "Pride™" Tush Tag (Est. Early 97) ④–**$625**

98

Mel™
8" • Koala • #4162 • Born: 1/15/96
Issued: 1/97 • Retired: 3/99
Market Value: ⑤–**$10** ④–**$15**

99

New!

Millenium™
10" • Bear • #4226 • Born: 1/1/99
Issued: 1/99 • Current
Market Value: ⑤–**$____**

BEANIE BABIES®

	Date Purchased	Tag Gen.	Price Paid	Value Of My Collection
96.				
97.				
98.				
99.				
PENCIL TOTALS				

BEANIE BABIES

100

New!

Mooch™
9" • Spider Monkey • #4224 • Born: 8/1/98
Issued: 1/99 • Current
Market Value: ⑤-$____

101

A

B

C

D

Mystic™
10" • Unicorn • #4007 • Born: 5/21/94
Issued: 6/94 • Current
Market Value:
A. Iridescent Horn/Fluffy Mane
(12/98-Current) ⑤-$____
B. Iridescent Horn/Coarse Mane
(10/97-12/98) ⑤-$12 ④-$19
C. Brown Horn/Coarse Mane
(Est. Late 95-10/97) ④-$35 ③-$135
D. Brown Horn/Fine Mane
(Est. 6/94-Late 95) ③-$285
②-$425 ①-$550

102

Nana™
(name changed to "Bongo™")
9" • Monkey • #4067 • Born: N/A
Issued: 6/95 • Retired: 1995
Market Value: ③-$4,050

103

Nanook™
10" • Husky • #4104 • Born: 11/21/96
Issued: 5/97 • Retired: 3/99
Market Value: ⑤-$12 ④-$16

BEANIE BABIES®

	Date Purchased	Tag Gen.	Price Paid	Value Of My Collection
100.				
101.				
102.				
103.				
104.				
PENCIL TOTALS				

104

New!

Nibbler™
8" • Bunny • #4216 • Born: 4/6/98
Issued: 1/99 • Current
Market Value: ⑤-$____

(105) New!

Nibbly™
8" • Bunny • #4217 • Born: 5/7/98
Issued: 1/99 • Current
Market Value: ⑤-$_____

(106)

A

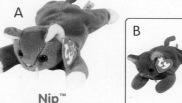

B

C

Nip™
10" • Cat • #4003 • Born: 3/6/94
Issued: 1/95 • Retired: 12/97
Market Value:
A. White Paws (2/96-12/97)
⑤-$28 ④-$28 ③-$300
B. All Gold (1/96-3/96) ③-$900
C. White Face (1/95-1/96)
③-$500 ②-$525

BEANIE BABIES®

(107)

Nuts™
8" • Squirrel • #4114 • Born: 1/21/96
Issued: 1/97 • Retired: 12/98
Market Value: ⑤-$12 ④-$15

(108)

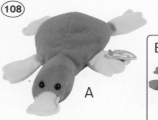

B

A

Patti™
10" • Platypus • #4025 • Born: 1/6/93
Issued: 1/94 • Retired: 5/98
Market Value:
A. Magenta (2/95-5/98) ⑤-$23
④-$27 ③-$235
B. Maroon (1/94-2/95) ③-$750
②-$875 ①-$1,000

(109)

Peace™
10" • Bear • #4053 • Born: 2/1/96
Issued: 5/97 • Current
Market Value: ⑤-$_____ ④-$40

BEANIE BABIES®

	Date Purchased	Tag Gen.	Price Paid	Value Of My Collection
105.				
106.				
107.				
108.				
109.				
PENCIL TOTALS				

110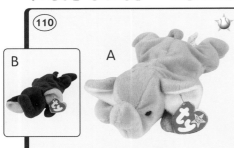

B

A

Peanut™
10" • Elephant • #4062 • Born: 1/25/95
Issued: 6/95 • Retired: 5/98
Market Value:
A. Light Blue (10/95-5/98) **5**–$23
4–$26 **3**–$925
B. Dark Blue (6/95-10/95) **3**–$4,800

111

Peking™
10" • Panda • #4013 • Born: N/A
Issued: 6/94 • Retired: 1/96
Market Value: **3**–$1,950
2–$2,100 **1**–$2,200

112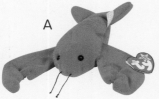

B

A

Pinchers™
10" • Lobster • #4026 • Born: 6/19/93
Issued: 1/94 • Retired: 5/98
Market Value:
A. "Pinchers™" Swing Tag (1/94-5/98) **5**–$24
4–$27 **3**–$125 **2**–$320 **1**–$575
B. "Punchers™" Swing Tag (Est. Early 94)
1–$3,400

113

Pinky™
10" • Flamingo • #4072 • Born: 2/13/95
Issued: 6/95 • Retired: 12/98
Market Value: **5**–$12 **4**–$15
3–$135

BEANIE BABIES®

	Date Purchased	Tag Gen.	Price Paid	Value Of My Collection
110.				
111.				
112.				
113.				
114.				
PENCIL TOTALS				

114

Pouch™
8" • Kangaroo • #4161 • Born: 11/6/96
Issued: 1/97 • Retired: 3/99
Market Value: **5**–$10 **4**–$14

BEANIE BABIES

(115)

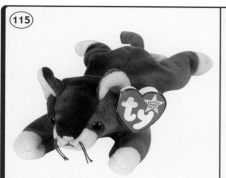

Pounce™
10" • Cat • #4122 • Born: 8/28/97
Issued: 12/97 • Retired: 3/99
Market Value: 5–**$10**

(116)

Prance™
10" • Cat • #4123 • Born: 11/20/97
Issued: 12/97 • Retired: 3/99
Market Value: 5–**$10**

(117)
New!

Prickles™
5" • Hedgehog • #4220 • Born: 2/19/98
Issued: 1/99 • Current
Market Value: 5–**$_____**

(118)

A

B

Princess™
10" • Bear • #4300 • Born: N/A
Issued: 10/97 • Current
Market Value:
A. "P.E. Pellets" On Tush Tag
(Est. Late 97-Current) 4–$_____
B. "P.V.C. Pellets" On Tush Tag
(Est. Late 97) 4–**$130**

(119)

Puffer™
9" • Puffin • #4181 • Born: 11/3/97
Issued: 12/97 • Retired: 9/98
Market Value: 5–**$13**

BEANIE BABIES®

	Date Purchased	Tag Gen.	Price Paid	Value Of My Collection
115.				
116.				
117.				
118.				
119.				
PENCIL TOTALS				

(120)

Pugsly™
10" • Pug Dog • #4106 • Born: 5/2/96
Issued: 5/97 • Retired: 3/99
Market Value: ⑤–$10 ④–$14

(121)

Pumkin'™
9" • Pumpkin • #4205 • Born: 10/31/98
Issued: 9/98 • Retired: 12/98
Market Value: ⑤–$35

(122)

B
A

Quackers™
8" • Duck • #4024 • Born: 4/19/94
Issued: 6/94 • Retired: 5/98
Market Value:
A. "Quackers™" With Wings (1/95-5/98)
⑤–$20 ④–$23 ③–$115 ②–$800
B. "Quacker™" Without Wings (6/94-1/95)
②–$2,100 ①–$2,300

(123)

Radar™
6" • Bat • #4091 • Born: 10/30/95
Issued: 9/95 • Retired: 5/97
Market Value: ④–$170 ③–$210

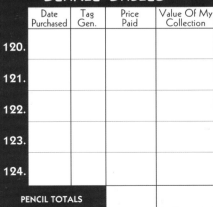

Beanie Babies®

	Date Purchased	Tag Gen.	Price Paid	Value Of My Collection
120.				
121.				
122.				
123.				
124.				
PENCIL TOTALS				

(124)

A

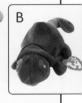

B

Rainbow™
10" • Chameleon • #4037 • Born: 10/14/97
Issued: 12/97 • Retired: 3/99
Market Value:
A. Tie-dye/With Tongue (Mid 98-3/99)
⑤–$15
B. Blue/No Tongue (12/97-Mid 98) ⑤–$20

(125)

Rex™
7" • Tyrannosaurus • #4086 • Born: N/A
Issued: 6/95 • Retired: 6/96
Market Value: ③–$925

(126)

Righty™
10" • Elephant • #4086 • Born: 7/4/96
Issued: 6/96 • Retired: 1/97
Market Value: ④–$275

(127)

Ringo™
12" • Raccoon • #4014 • Born: 7/14/95
Issued: 1/96 • Retired: 9/98
Market Value: ⑤–$15 ④–$18 ③–$95

(128)

Roam™
8" • Buffalo • #4209 • Born: 9/27/98
Issued: 9/98 • Current
Market Value: ⑤–$____

(129)

Roary™
10" • Lion • #4069 • Born: 2/20/96
Issued: 5/97 • Retired: 12/98
Market Value: ⑤–$13 ④–$16

BEANIE BABIES®

	Date Purchased	Tag Gen.	Price Paid	Value Of My Collection
125.				
126.				
127.				
128.				
129.				
PENCIL TOTALS				

(130)

Rocket™
9" • Blue Jay • #4202 • Born: 3/12/97
Issued: 5/98 • Current
Market Value: ⑤-$_____

(131)

Rover™
8" • Dog • #4101 • Born: 5/30/96
Issued: 6/96 • Retired: 5/98
Market Value: ⑤-$23 ④-$27

(132) *New!*

Sammy™
10" • Bear • #4215 • Born: 6/23/98
Issued: 1/99 • Current
Market Value: ⑤-$_____

(133)

Santa™
9" • Elf • #4203 • Born: 12/6/98
Issued: 9/98 • Retired: 12/98
Market Value: ⑤-$35

BEANIE BABIES®

	Date Purchased	Tag Gen.	Price Paid	Value Of My Collection
130.				
131.				
132.				
133.				
134.				
PENCIL TOTALS				

(134) *New!*

Scat™
10" • Cat • #4231 • Born: 5/27/98
Issued: 1/99 • Current
Market Value: ⑤-$_____

BEANIE BABIES®

(135)

Scoop™
8" • Pelican • #4107 • Born: 7/1/96
Issued: 6/96 • Retired: 12/98
Market Value: ⑤–**$12** ④–**$16**

(136)

Scorch™
11" • Dragon • #4210 • Born: 7/31/98
Issued: 9/98 • Current
Market Value: ⑤–$_____

(137)

Scottie™
8" • Scottish Terrier • #4102
Born: 6/3/96 or 6/15/96
Issued: 6/96 • Retired: 5/98
Market Value: ⑤–**$25** ④–**$30**

(138)

Seamore™
8" • Seal • #4029 • Born: 12/14/96
Issued: 6/94 • Retired: 10/97
Market Value: ④–**$150** ③–**$210**
②–**$370** ①–**$540**

(139)

Seaweed™
8" • Otter • #4080 • Born: 3/19/96
Issued: 1/96 • Retired: 9/98
Market Value: ⑤–**$28** ④–**$32** ③–**$105**

BEANIE BABIES®

	Date Purchased	Tag Gen.	Price Paid	Value Of My Collection
135.				
136.				
137.				
138.				
139.				
PENCIL TOTALS				

93

(140)

New!

Slippery™
10" • Seal • #4222 • Born: 1/17/98
Issued: 1/99 • Current
Market Value: ⑤-$_____

(141)

Slither™
23" • Snake • #4031 • Born: N/A
Issued: 6/94 • Retired: 6/95
Market Value: ③-$1,900
②-$2,000 ①-$2,200

(142)

A

B

Sly™
10" • Fox • #4115 • Born: 9/12/96
Issued: 6/96 • Retired: 9/98
Market Value:
A. White Belly (8/96-9/98) ⑤-$13 ④-$16
B. Brown Belly (6/96-8/96) ④-$160

(143)

Smoochy™
10" • Frog • #4039 • Born: 10/1/97
Issued: 12/97 • Retired: 3/99
Market Value: ⑤-$10

Beanie Babies®

	Date Purchased	Tag Gen.	Price Paid	Value Of My Collection
140.				
141.				
142.				
143.				
144.				
PENCIL TOTALS				

(144)

Snip™
10" • Siamese Cat • #4120 • Born: 10/22/96
Issued: 1/97 • Retired: 12/98
Market Value: ⑤-$13 ④-$16

(145)

Snort™
10" • Bull • #4002 • Born: 5/15/95
Issued: 1/97 • Retired: 9/98
Market Value: ⑤–$13 ④–$16

(146)

Snowball™
8" • Snowman • #4201 • Born: 12/22/96
Issued: 10/97 • Retired: 12/97
Market Value: ④–$44

(147)

Sparky™
10" • Dalmatian • #4100 • Born: 2/27/96
Issued: 6/96 • Retired: 5/97
Market Value: ④–$140

(148)

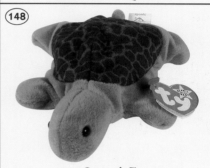

Speedy™
7" • Turtle • #4030 • Born: 8/14/94
Issued: 6/94 • Retired: 10/97
Market Value: ④–$35 ③–$125
②–$250 ①–$400

(149)

Spike™
10" • Rhinoceros • #4060 • Born: 8/13/96
Issued: 6/96 • Retired: 12/98
Market Value: ⑤–$12 ④–$15

BEANIE BABIES®

	Date Purchased	Tag Gen.	Price Paid	Value Of My Collection
145.				
146.				
147.				
148.				
149.				
PENCIL TOTALS				

BEANIE BABIES®

95

VALUE GUIDE - BEANIE BABIES®

(150)

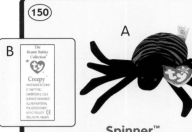
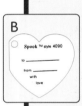

Spinner™
8" • Spider • #4036 • Born: 10/28/96
Issued: 10/97 • Retired: 9/98
Market Value:
A. "Spinner™" Tush Tag (10/97-9/98)
⑤–**$13** ④–**$17**
B. "Creepy™" Tush Tag (Est. Late 97-9/98)
⑤–**$55**

(151)

Splash™
10" • Whale • #4022 • Born: 7/8/93
Issued: 1/94 • Retired: 5/97
Market Value: ④–**$120** ③–**$185**
②–**$350** ①–**$500**

(152)

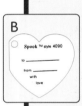

Spooky™
8" • Ghost • #4090 • Born: 10/31/95
Issued: 9/95 • Retired: 12/97
Market Value:
A. "Spooky™" Swing Tag (Est. Late 95-12/97)
④–**$40** ③–**$160**
B. "Spook™" Swing Tag (Est. 9/95-Late 95)
③–**$450**

(153)

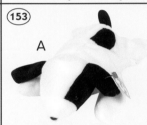

Spot™
10" • Dog • #4000 • Born: 1/3/93
Issued: 1/94 • Retired: 10/97
Market Value:
A. With Spot (4/94-10/97)
④–**$55** ③–**$140** ②–**$750**
B. Without Spot (1/94-4/94)
②–**$1,900** ①–**$2,150**

BEANIE BABIES®

	Date Purchased	Tag Gen.	Price Paid	Value Of My Collection
150.				
151.				
152.				
153.				
154.				
PENCIL TOTALS				

(154)

Spunky™
10" • Cocker Spaniel • #4184 • Born: 1/14/97
Issued: 12/97 • Retired: 3/99
Market Value: ⑤–**$12**

(155)

Squealer™
10" • Pig • #4005 • Born: 4/23/93
Issued: 1/94 • Retired: 5/98
Market Value: ⑤–$28 ④–$32
③–$110 ②–$270 ①–$420

(156)

Steg™
9" • Stegosaurus • #4087 • Born: N/A
Issued: 6/95 • Retired: 6/96
Market Value: ③–$1,000

(157)

New!

Stilts™
12" • Stork • #4221 • Born: 6/16/98
Issued: 1/99 • Current
Market Value: ⑤–$_____

(158)

Sting™
10" • Stingray • #4077 • Born: 8/27/95
Issued: 6/95 • Retired: 1/97
Market Value: ④–$175 ③–$245

BEANIE BABIES®

	Date Purchased	Tag Gen.	Price Paid	Value Of My Collection
155.				
156.				
157.				
158.				
PENCIL TOTALS				

BEANIE BABIES®

(159)

Stinger™
12" • Scorpion • #4193 • Born: 9/29/97
Issued: 5/98 • Retired: 12/98
Market Value: ⑤–$14

(160)

Stinky™
10" • Skunk • #4017 • Born: 2/13/95
Issued: 6/95 • Current
Market Value: ⑤–$15 ④–$18 ③–$95

(161)

Stretch™
12" • Ostrich • #4182 • Born: 9/21/97
Issued: 12/97 • Retired: 3/99
Market Value: ⑤–$10

(162)

A

Stripes™
10" • Tiger • #4065 • Born: 6/11/95
Issued: Est. 6/95 • Retired: 5/98
Market Value:
A. Light w/Fewer Stripes
(6/96-5/98) ⑤–$18 ④–$22
B. Dark w/Fuzzy Belly
(Est. Early 96-6/96) ③–$1,100
C. Dark w/More Stripes
(Est. 6/95-Early 96) ③–$400

B

C

BEANIE BABIES®

	Date Purchased	Tag Gen.	Price Paid	Value Of My Collection
159.				
160.				
161.				
162.				
163.				
PENCIL TOTALS				

(163)

Strut™
(name changed from "Doodle™")
8" • Rooster • #4171 • Born: 3/8/96
Issued: 7/97 • Retired: 3/99
Market Value: ⑤–$10 ④–$16

(164)

Tabasco™
10" • Bull • #4002 • Born: 5/15/95
Issued: 6/95 • Retired: 1/97
Market Value: ❹–$180 ❸–$225

(165)

A

B

C

Tank™
9" • Armadillo • #4031 • Born: 2/22/95
Issued: Est. 1/96 • Retired: 10/97
Market Value:
A. 9 Plates/With Shell
(Est. Late 96-10/97) ❹–$80
B. 9 Plates/Without Shell
(Est. Mid 96-Late 96) ❹–$215
C. 7 Plates/Without Shell
(Est. 1/96-Mid 96) ❸–$190

(166)

B

A

Teddy™ (brown)
10" • Bear • #4050 • Born: 11/28/95
Issued: 6/94 • Retired: 10/97
Market Value:
A. New Face (1/95-10/97) ❹–$100
❸–$375 ❷–$800
B. Old Face (6/94-1/95) ❷–$2,600 ❶–$2,800

(167)

A

B

Teddy™ (cranberry)
10" • Bear • #4052 • Born: N/A
Issued: 6/94 • Retired: 1/96
Market Value:
A. New Face (1/95-1/96) ❸–$1,800 ❷–$1,900
B. Old Face (6/94-1/95) ❷–$1,800 ❶–$1,900

(168)

B

A

Teddy™ (jade)
10" • Bear • #4057 • Born: N/A
Issued: 6/94 • Retired: 1/96
Market Value:
A. New Face (1/95-1/96) ❸–$1,800 ❷–$1,900
B. Old Face (6/94-1/95) ❷–$1,800 ❶–$1,900

BEANIE BABIES®

	Date Purchased	Tag Gen.	Price Paid	Value Of My Collection
164.				
165.				
166.				
167.				
168.				
PENCIL TOTALS				

(169)

B **A**

Teddy™ (magenta)
10" • Bear • #4056 • Born: N/A
Issued: 6/94 • Retired: 1/96
Market Value:
A. New Face (1/95-1/96) ③–**$1,800** ②–**$1,900**
B. Old Face (6/94-1/95) ②–**$1,800** ①–**$1,900**

(170)

A **B**

Teddy™ (teal)
10" • Bear • #4051 • Born: N/A
Issued: 6/94 • Retired: 1/96
Market Value:
A. New Face (1/95-1/96) ③–**$1,800** ②–**$1,900**
B. Old Face (6/94-1/95) ②–**$1,800** ①–**$1,900**

(171)

B **A**

C

Teddy™ (violet)
10" • Bear • #4055 • Born: N/A
Issued: 6/94 • Retired: 1/96
Market Value:
A. New Face (1/95-1/96)
③–**$1,800** ②–**$1,900**
B. New Face/Employee Bear w/Red
Tush Tag (Green or Red Ribbon)
No Swing Tag – **$4,000**
C. Old Face (6/94-1/95)
②–**$1,800** ①–**$1,900**

(172)

New!

Tiny™
8" • Chihuahua • #4234 • Born: 9/8/98
Issued: 1/99 • Current
Market Value: ⑤–**$_____**

Beanie Babies®

	Date Purchased	Tag Gen.	Price Paid	Value Of My Collection
169.				
170.				
171.				
172.				
173.				
PENCIL TOTALS				

(173)

Tracker™
9" • Basset Hound • #4198 • Born: 6/5/97
Issued: 5/98 • Current
Market Value: ⑤–**$_____**

(174)

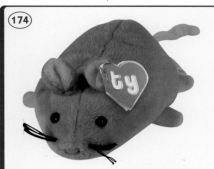

Trap™
9" • Mouse • #4042 • Born: N/A
Issued: 6/94 • Retired: 6/95
Market Value: ❸–**$1,500**
❷–**$1,600** ❶–**$1,750**

(175)

Tuffy™
10" • Terrier • #4108 • Born: 10/12/96
Issued: 5/97 • Retired: 12/98
Market Value: ❺–**$12** ❹–**$16**

(176)

A

B

Tusk™
8" • Walrus • #4076 • Born: 9/18/95
Issued: Est. 6/95 • Retired: 1/97
Market Value:
A. "Tusk™" Swing Tag (6/95-1/97)
❹–**$140** ❸–**$195**
B. "Tuck™" Swing Tag (Est. Early 96-1/97) ❹–**$155**

(177)

Twigs™
9" • Giraffe • #4068 • Born: 5/19/95
Issued: 1/96 • Retired: 5/98
Market Value: ❺–**$23** ❹–**$25** ❸–**$110**

BEANIE BABIES®

	Date Purchased	Tag Gen.	Price Paid	Value Of My Collection
174.				
175.				
176.				
177.				
PENCIL TOTALS				

178 New!

Valentina™
10" • Bear • #4233 • Born: 2/14/98
Issued: 1/99 • Current
Market Value: ⑤–$_____

179

Valentino™
10" • Bear • #4058 • Born: 2/14/94
Issued: 1/95 • Retired: 12/98
Market Value: ⑤–$28 ④–$32
③–$145 ②–$260

180

Velvet™
10" • Panther • #4064 • Born: 12/16/95
Issued: 6/95 • Retired: 10/97
Market Value: ④–$35 ③–$110

181

Waddle™
10" • Penguin • #4075 • Born: 12/19/95
Issued: 6/95 • Retired: 5/98
Market Value: ⑤–$25 ④–$28 ③–$100

BEANIE BABIES®

	Date Purchased	Tag Gen.	Price Paid	Value Of My Collection
178.				
179.				
180.				
181.				
182.				
PENCIL TOTALS				

182

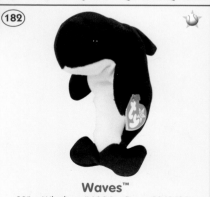

Waves™
10" • Whale • #4084 • Born: 12/8/96
Issued: 5/97 • Retired: 5/98
Market Value: ⑤–$22 ④–$26

BEANIE BABIES®

(183)

Web™
10" • Spider • #4041 • Born: N/A
Issued: 6/94 • Retired: 1/96
Market Value: ③–**$1,300**
②–**$1,400** ①–**$1,600**

(184)

Weenie™
9" • Dachshund • #4013 • Born: 7/20/95
Issued: 1/96 • Retired: 5/98
Market Value: ⑤–**$30** ④–**$34** ③–**$120**

(185)

Whisper™
8" • Deer • #4194 • Born: 4/5/97
Issued: 5/98 • Current
Market Value: ⑤–**$_____**

(186)

Wise™
9" • Owl • #4187 • Born: 5/31/97
Issued: 5/98 • Retired: 12/98
Market Value: ⑤–**$27**

(187)

Wrinkles™
10" • Bulldog • #4103 • Born: 5/1/96
Issued: 6/96 • Retired: 9/98
Market Value: ⑤–**$15** ④–**$18**

BEANIE BABIES®

	Date Purchased	Tag Gen.	Price Paid	Value Of My Collection
183.				
184.				
185.				
186.				
187.				
PENCIL TOTALS				

VALUE GUIDE - BEANIE BABIES®

188

Zero™
6" • Penguin • #4207 • Born: 1/2/98
Issued: 9/98 • Retired: 12/98
Market Value: ⑤–$30

189

Ziggy™
10" • Zebra • #4063 • Born: 12/24/95
Issued: 6/95 • Retired: 5/98
Market Value: ⑤–$23 ④–$26 ③–$105

190

B
C

A

Zip™
10" • Cat • #4004 • Born: 3/28/94
Issued: 1/95 • Retired: 5/98
Market Value:
A. White Paws (3/96-5/98)
⑤–$38 ④–$42 ③–$425
B. All Black (1/96-3/96)
③–$1,300
C. White Face (1/95-1/96)
③–$485 ②–$525

BEANIE BABIES®

	Date Purchased	Tag Gen.	Price Paid	Value Of My Collection
188.				
189.				
190.				
PENCIL TOTALS				

Value Guide - Future Releases

Use these pages to record future Beanie Babies® releases.

Beanie Babies®	Date Purchased	Tag Gen.	Price Paid	Value Of My Collection
		PENCIL TOTALS		

VALUE GUIDE - FUTURE RELEASES

Use these pages to record future Beanie Babies® releases.

BEANIE BABIES®	Date Purchased	Tag Gen.	Price Paid	Value Of My Collection
		PENCIL TOTALS		

VALUE GUIDE - BEANIE BABIES®

SPORTS PROMOTION BEANIE BABIES®

Since 1997, the cuddly *Beanie Babies* have been featured in numerous promotions on fields, courts and rinks all across North America, helping to cheer on their favorite teams.

SPORTS PROMOTION BEANIE BABIES® KEY

Canadian Special Olympics		National Football League	
Major League Baseball		National Hockey League	
National Basketball Association		Women's National Basketball Association	

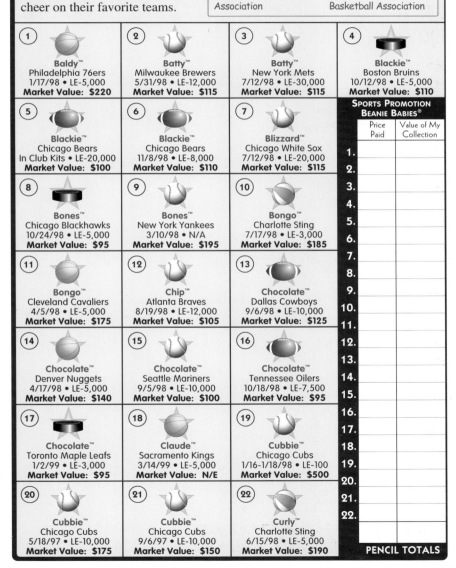

1 — **Baldy™**
Philadelphia 76ers
1/17/98 • LE-5,000
Market Value: $220

2 — **Batty™**
Milwaukee Brewers
5/31/98 • LE-12,000
Market Value: $115

3 — **Batty™**
New York Mets
7/12/98 • LE-30,000
Market Value: $115

4 — **Blackie™**
Boston Bruins
10/12/98 • LE-5,000
Market Value: $110

5 — **Blackie™**
Chicago Bears
In Club Kits • LE-20,000
Market Value: $100

6 — **Blackie™**
Chicago Bears
11/8/98 • LE-8,000
Market Value: $110

7 — **Blizzard™**
Chicago White Sox
7/12/98 • LE-20,000
Market Value: $115

8 — **Bones™**
Chicago Blackhawks
10/24/98 • LE-5,000
Market Value: $95

9 — **Bones™**
New York Yankees
3/10/98 • N/A
Market Value: $195

10 — **Bongo™**
Charlotte Sting
7/17/98 • LE-3,000
Market Value: $185

11 — **Bongo™**
Cleveland Cavaliers
4/5/98 • LE-5,000
Market Value: $175

12 — **Chip™**
Atlanta Braves
8/19/98 • LE-12,000
Market Value: $105

13 — **Chocolate™**
Dallas Cowboys
9/6/98 • LE-10,000
Market Value: $125

14 — **Chocolate™**
Denver Nuggets
4/17/98 • LE-5,000
Market Value: $140

15 — **Chocolate™**
Seattle Mariners
9/5/98 • LE-10,000
Market Value: $100

16 — **Chocolate™**
Tennessee Oilers
10/18/98 • LE-7,500
Market Value: $95

17 — **Chocolate™**
Toronto Maple Leafs
1/2/99 • LE-3,000
Market Value: $95

18 — **Claude™**
Sacramento Kings
3/14/99 • LE-5,000
Market Value: N/E

19 — **Cubbie™**
Chicago Cubs
1/16-1/18/98 • LE-100
Market Value: $500

20 — **Cubbie™**
Chicago Cubs
5/18/97 • LE-10,000
Market Value: $175

21 — **Cubbie™**
Chicago Cubs
9/6/97 • LE-10,000
Market Value: $150

22 — **Curly™**
Charlotte Sting
6/15/98 • LE-5,000
Market Value: $190

SPORTS PROMOTION BEANIE BABIES®

	Price Paid	Value of My Collection
1.		
2.		
3.		
4.		
5.		
6.		
7.		
8.		
9.		
10.		
11.		
12.		
13.		
14.		
15.		
16.		
17.		
18.		
19.		
20.		
21.		
22.		
PENCIL TOTALS		

BEANIE BABIES®

VALUE GUIDE - BEANIE BABIES®

No.	Name	Team	Date • Edition	Market Value
23	Curly™	Chicago Bears	12/20/98 • LE-10,000	$100
24	Curly™	Cleveland Rockers	8/15/98 • LE-3,200	$140
25	Curly™	New York Mets	8/22/98 • LE-30,000	$95
26	Curly™	San Antonio Spurs	4/27/98 • LE-2,500	$155
27	Daisy™	Chicago Cubs	5/3/98 • LE-10,000	$375
28	Derby™	Houston Astros	8/16/98 • LE-15,000	$105
29	Derby™	Indianapolis Colts	10/4/98 • LE-10,000	$100
30	Dotty™	Los Angeles Sparks	7/31/98 • LE-3,000	$155
31	Ears™	Oakland A's	3/15/98 • LE-1,500	$240
32	Erin™	Chicago Cubs	8/5/99 • LE-12,000	N/E
33	Glory™	All-Star Game	7/7/98 • LE-52,000 approx.	$190
34	Goatee™	Arizona Diamondbacks	7/8/99 • LE-10,000	N/E
35	Gobbles™	Phoenix Coyotes	11/26/98 • LE-5,000	$95
36	Gobbles™	St. Louis Blues	11/24/98 • LE-7,500	$95
37	Gracie™	Chicago Cubs	9/13/98 • LE-10,000	$135
38	Hippie™	St. Louis Blues	3/22/99 • LE-7,500	N/E
39	Hissy™	Arizona Diamondbacks	6/14/98 • LE-6,500	$90
40	Lucky™	Minnesota Twins	7/31/98 • LE-10,000	$110
41	Mac™	St. Louis Cardinals	6/14/99 • LE-20,000	N/E
42	Maple™	Canadian Special Olympics	8/97 & 12/97 • N/A	$400
43	Mel™	Anaheim Angels	9/6/98 • LE-10,000	$115
44	Mel™	Detroit Shock	7/25/98 • LE-5,000	$125
45	Millenium™	Chicago Cubs	9/26/99 • LE-40,000	N/E
46	Mystic™	Los Angeles Sparks	8/3/98 • LE-5,000	$130
47	Mystic™	Washington Mystics	7/11/98 • LE-5,000	$160
48	Peanut™	Oakland A's	8/1/98 • LE-15,000	$95
49	Peanut™	Oakland A's	9/6/98 • LE-15,000	$95
50	Pinky™	San Antonio Spurs	4/29/98 • LE-2,500	$150
51	Pinky™	Tampa Bay Devil Rays	8/23/98 • LE-10,000	$80
52	Pugsly™	Atlanta Braves	9/2/98 • LE-12,000	$90

SPORTS PROMOTION BEANIE BABIES®

	Price Paid	Value of My Collection
23.		
24.		
25.		
26.		
27.		
28.		
29.		
30.		
31.		
32.		
33.		
34.		
35.		
36.		
37.		
38.		
39.		
40.		
41.		
42.		
43.		
44.		
45.		
46.		
47.		
48.		
49.		
50.		
51.		
52.		
PENCIL TOTALS		

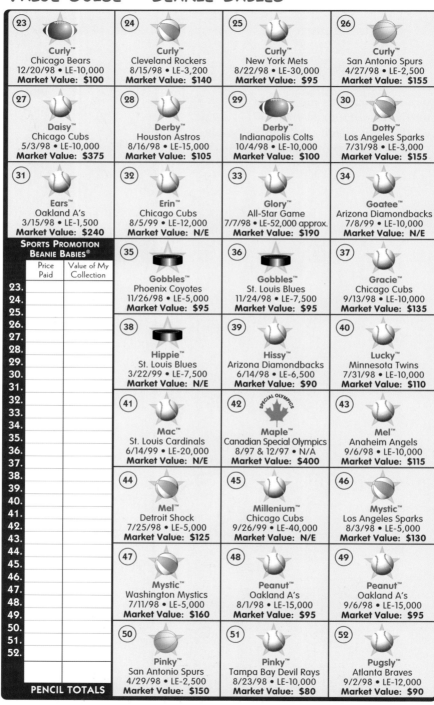

BEANIE BABIES®

53 Pugsly™ Texas Rangers 8/4/98 • LE-10,000 **Market Value: $110**	**54** Roam™ Buffalo Sabres 2/19/99 • LE-5,000 **Market Value: N/E**	**55** Roary™ Kansas City Royals 5/31/98 • LE-13,000 **Market Value: $100**	**56** Rocket™ Toronto Blue Jays 9/6/98 • LE-12,000 **Market Value: $110**
57 Rover™ Cincinnati Reds 8/16/98 • LE-15,000 **Market Value: $85**	**58** Sammy™ Chicago Cubs 4/25/99 • LE-12,000 **Market Value: N/E**	**59** Scoop™ Houston Comets 8/6/98 • LE-5,000 **Market Value: $150**	**60** Sly™ Arizona Diamondbacks 8/27/98 • LE-10,000 **Market Value: $90**
61 Smoochy™ St. Louis Cardinals 8/14/98 • LE-20,000 **Market Value: $110**	**62** Spunky™ Buffalo Sabres 10/23/98 • LE-5,000 **Market Value: $90**	**63** Stretch™ New York Yankees 8/9/98 • N/A **Market Value: $100**	**64** Stretch™ St. Louis Cardinals 5/22/98 • LE-20,000 **Market Value: $105**

65 Stripes™ Detroit Tigers 5/31/98 • LE-10,000 **Market Value: $100**	**66** Stripes™ Detroit Tigers 8/8/98 • LE-10,000 **Market Value: $95**	**67** Strut™ Indiana Pacers 4/2/98 • LE-5,000 **Market Value: $120**	
68 Tiny™ Houston Astros 7/18/99 • LE-20,000 **Market Value: N/E**	**69** Tuffy™ New Jersey Devils 10/24/98 • LE-5,000 **Market Value: $100**	**70** Tuffy™ San Francisco Giants 8/30/98 • LE-10,000 **Market Value: $100**	
71 Valentino™ Canadian Special Olympics 6/98, 9/98 & 10/98 • N/A **Market Value: $240**	**72** Valentino™ New York Yankees 5/17/98 • LE-10,000 **Market Value: $175**	**73** Waddle™ Pittsburgh Penguins 10/24/98 • LE-7,000 **Market Value: $85**	
74 Waddle™ Pittsburgh Penguins 11/21/98 • LE-7,000 **Market Value: $85**	**75** Waves™ San Diego Padres 8/14/98 • LE-10,000 **Market Value: $105**	**76** Weenie™ Tampa Bay Devil Rays 7/26/98 • LE-15,000 **Market Value: $95**	

SPORTS PROMOTION BEANIE BABIES®

	Price Paid	Value of My Collection
53.		
54.		
55.		
56.		
57.		
58.		
59.		
60.		
61.		
62.		
63.		
64.		
65.		
66.		
67.		
68.		
69.		
70.		
71.		
72.		
73.		
74.		
75.		
76.		
PENCIL TOTALS		

Stay tuned for more upcoming *Beanie Babies* promotions:

San Francisco Giants 4/11/99
Oakland A's 5/1/99
New York Yankees 5/9/99
Seattle Mariners 5/29/99
Kansas City Royals 6/6/99
Cincinnati Reds 6/19/99
New York Yankees 8/15/99

BUDDIES FOR LIFE

The *Beanie Buddies* collection, the newest member of the Ty plush family, more than doubled in size with the introduction of 14 new pieces in early 1999, bringing the total number of pieces to 23. The line also saw its first retirements when "Twigs" retired on December 31, 1998 and "Beak" retired on March 31, 1999. These popular characters, larger than their *Beanie Baby* counterparts and made from a special fabric called "Tylon," have been an instant hit with Ty plush collectors.

(1)

Beak™
12" • Kiwi • #9301
Issued: 9/98 • Retired: 3/99
Market Value: $50

(2) New!

Bongo™
13" • Monkey • #9312
Issued: 1/99 • Current
Market Value: $_____

BEANIE BUDDIES®

	Date Purchased	Price Paid	Value Of My Collection
1.			
2.			
3.			
PENCIL TOTALS			

(3) New!

Bubbles™
13" • Fish • #9323
Issued: 1/99 • Current
Market Value: $_____

BEANIE BUDDIES®

④ New!

Chilly™
16" • Polar Bear • #9317
Issued: 1/99 • Current
Market Value: $_____

⑤ New!

Chip™
16" • Cat • #9318
Issued: 1/99 • Current
Market Value: $_____

⑥ New!

Erin™
16" • Bear • #9309
Issued: 1/99 • Current
Market Value: $_____

⑦ New!

Hippity™
12" • Bunny • #9324
Issued: 1/99 • Current
Market Value: $_____

BEANIE BUDDIES®

	Date Purchased	Price Paid	Value Of My Collection
4.			
5.			
6.			
7.			
PENCIL TOTALS			

8

Humphrey™
13" • Camel • #9307
Issued: 9/98 • Current
Market Value: $_____

9

Jake™
12" • Mallard Duck • #9304
Issued: 9/98 • Current
Market Value: $_____

10

 New!

Patti™
13" • Platypus • #9320
Issued: 1/99 • Current
Market Value: $_____

11

Peanut™
16" • Elephant • #9300
Issued: 9/98 • Current
Market Value: $_____

BEANIE BUDDIES®

	Date Purchased	Price Paid	Value Of My Collection
8.			
9.			
10.			
11.			
12.			
PENCIL TOTALS			

12 New!

Peking™
16" • Panda • #9310
Issued: 1/99 • Current
Market Value: $_____

(13) New!

Pinky™
16" • Flamingo • #9316
Issued: 1/99 • Current
Market Value: $_____

(14)

Quackers™
12" • Duck • #9302
Issued: 9/98 • Current
Market Value: $_____

(15)

Rover™
13" • Dog • #9305
Issued: 9/98 • Current
Market Value: $_____

(16) New!

Smoochy™
13" • Frog • #9315
Issued: 1/99 • Current
Market Value: $_____

BEANIE BUDDIES®

BEANIE BUDDIES®

	Date Purchased	Price Paid	Value Of My Collection
13.			
14.			
15.			
16.			
PENCIL TOTALS			

(17) New!

Snort™
16" • Bull • #9311
Issued: 1/99 • Current
Market Value: $_____

(18) New!

Squealer™
16" • Pig • #9313
Issued: 1/99 • Current
Market Value: $_____

(19)

Stretch™
16" • Ostrich • #9303
Issued: 9/98 • Current
Market Value: $_____

(20)

Teddy™
16" • Bear • #9306
Issued: 9/98 • Current
Market Value: $_____

BEANIE BUDDIES®

	Date Purchased	Price Paid	Value Of My Collection
17.			
18.			
19.			
20.			
21.			
PENCIL TOTALS			

(21) New!

Tracker™
13" • Basset Hound • #9319
Issued: 1/99 • Current
Market Value: $_____

22

Twigs™
13" • Giraffe • #9308
Issued: 9/98 • Retired: 12/98
Market Value: $125

23

New!

Waddle™
12" • Penguin • #9314
Issued: 1/99 • Current
Market Value: $_____

24

Mystery Beanie Buddies®
Release
Coming Soon!
Market Value: $_____

BEANIE BUDDIES®

BEANIE BUDDIES®

	Date Purchased	Price Paid	Value Of My Collection
22.			
23.			
24.			
PENCIL TOTALS			

Value Guide - Future Releases

Use this page to record future Beanie Buddies® releases.

Beanie Buddies®	Date Purchased	Price Paid	Value Of My Collection
PENCIL TOTALS			

A "TEENIE" FEEDING FRENZY

In April 1997, McDonald's fast-food restaurants served up 10 tiny versions of the popular *Beanie Babies* in a highly successful promotion. The response was overwhelming and the pieces "sold out" in a much shorter time than anticipated. So in May 1998, the company ran a second promotion, this time with 12 *Teenie Beanie Babies* who found their way into Happy Meals and happy collectors' homes across the country. Despite reports that a much larger quantity was produced for the second promotion, the supply of *Teenie Beanie Babies* still ran out quickly.

①

1997 Teenie Beanie Babies™ Complete Set (set/10)
Issued: 4/97 • Retired: 5/97
Market Value: $175

②

1998 Teenie Beanie Babies™ Complete Set (set/12)
Issued: 5/98 • Retired: 6/98
Market Value: $70

③

Bones™
6" • Dog
2nd Promotion, #9 of 12
Issued: 5/98 • Retired: 6/98
Market Value: $7

④

Bongo™
5" • Monkey
2nd Promotion, #2 of 12
Issued: 5/98 • Retired: 6/98
Market Value: $14

⑤

Chocolate™
5.5" • Moose
1st Promotion, #4 of 10
Issued: 4/97 • Retired: 5/97
Market Value: $30

TEENIE BEANIE BABIES™

	Price Paid	Value Of My Collection
1.		
2.		
3.		
4.		
5.		
PENCIL TOTALS		

TEENIE BEANIE BABIES™

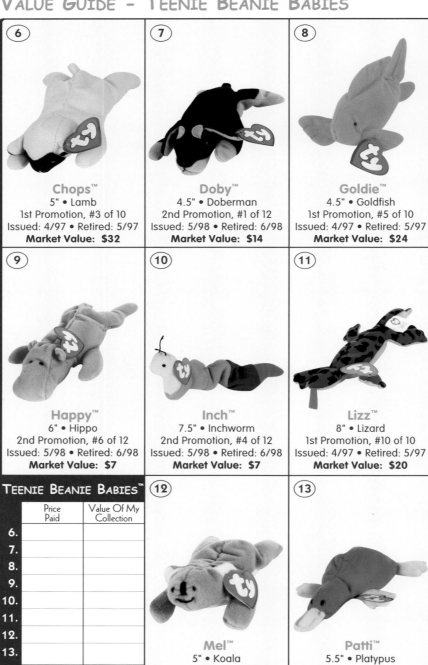

(6)

Chops™
5" • Lamb
1st Promotion, #3 of 10
Issued: 4/97 • Retired: 5/97
Market Value: $32

(7)

Doby™
4.5" • Doberman
2nd Promotion, #1 of 12
Issued: 5/98 • Retired: 6/98
Market Value: $14

(8)

Goldie™
4.5" • Goldfish
1st Promotion, #5 of 10
Issued: 4/97 • Retired: 5/97
Market Value: $24

(9)

Happy™
6" • Hippo
2nd Promotion, #6 of 12
Issued: 5/98 • Retired: 6/98
Market Value: $7

(10)

Inch™
7.5" • Inchworm
2nd Promotion, #4 of 12
Issued: 5/98 • Retired: 6/98
Market Value: $7

(11)

Lizz™
8" • Lizard
1st Promotion, #10 of 10
Issued: 4/97 • Retired: 5/97
Market Value: $20

TEENIE BEANIE BABIES™

	Price Paid	Value Of My Collection
6.		
7.		
8.		
9.		
10.		
11.		
12.		
13.		
PENCIL TOTALS		

(12)

Mel™
5" • Koala
2nd Promotion, #7 of 12
Issued: 5/98 • Retired: 6/98
Market Value: $7

(13)

Patti™
5.5" • Platypus
1st Promotion, #1 of 10
Issued: 4/97 • Retired: 5/97
Market Value: $36

118

14

Peanut™
6" • Elephant
2nd Promotion, #12 of 12
Issued: 5/98 • Retired: 6/98
Market Value: $7

15

Pinchers™
6.5" • Lobster
2nd Promotion, #5 of 12
Issued: 5/98 • Retired: 6/98
Market Value: $7

16

Pinky™
7" • Flamingo
1st Promotion, #2 of 10
Issued: 4/97 • Retired: 5/97
Market Value: $45

17

Quacks™
3.5" • Duck
1st Promotion, #9 of 10
Issued: 4/97 • Retired: 5/97
Market Value: $17

18

Scoop™
4" • Pelican
2nd Promotion, #8 of 12
Issued: 5/98 • Retired: 6/98
Market Value: $7

19

Seamore™
4.5" • Seal
1st Promotion, #7 of 10
Issued: 4/97 • Retired: 5/97
Market Value: $28

20

Snort™
6" • Bull
1st Promotion, #8 of 10
Issued: 4/97 • Retired: 5/97
Market Value: $15

21

Speedy™
4" • Turtle
1st Promotion, #6 of 10
Issued: 4/97 • Retired: 5/97
Market Value: $24

TEENIE BEANIE BABIES™

	Price Paid	Value Of My Collection
14.		
15.		
16.		
17.		
18.		
19.		
20.		
21.		
PENCIL TOTALS		

TEENIE BEANIE BABIES™

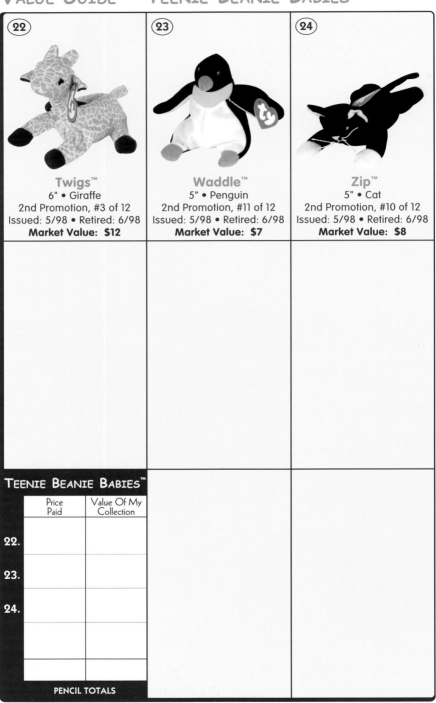

(22)

Twigs™
6" • Giraffe
2nd Promotion, #3 of 12
Issued: 5/98 • Retired: 6/98
Market Value: $12

(23)

Waddle™
5" • Penguin
2nd Promotion, #11 of 12
Issued: 5/98 • Retired: 6/98
Market Value: $7

(24)

Zip™
5" • Cat
2nd Promotion, #10 of 12
Issued: 5/98 • Retired: 6/98
Market Value: $8

TEENIE BEANIE BABIES™

	Price Paid	Value Of My Collection
22.		
23.		
24.		
PENCIL TOTALS		

Use this page to record future Teenie Beanie Babies™ releases.

TEENIE BEANIE BABIES™	Date Purchased	Price Paid	Value Of My Collection
PENCIL TOTALS			

TEENIE BEANIE BABIES™

Plenty Of Playful Pillow Pals™

Ty has quite a few surprises for *Pillow Pals* fans in 1999! A total of 15 new, vibrantly colored pieces have been introduced in the collection in early 1999, many of which are versions of old *Pillow Pal* favorites, while others are brand new friends. When these new colorful counterparts were introduced, the original members of this fluffy family headed off into retirement, dramatically raising the number of retired pieces in the collection to 28.

①

Antlers™
14" • Moose • #3028
Issued: 1998 • Retired: 1998
Market Value: $25

② New!

Antlers™
14" • Moose • #3104
Issued: 1999 • Current
Market Value: $_____

Pillow Pals™

	Date Purchased	Price Paid	Value Of My Collection
1.			
2.			
3.			
PENCIL TOTALS			

③

Ba Ba™
15" • Lamb • #3008
Issued: 1997 • Retired: 1998
Market Value: $14

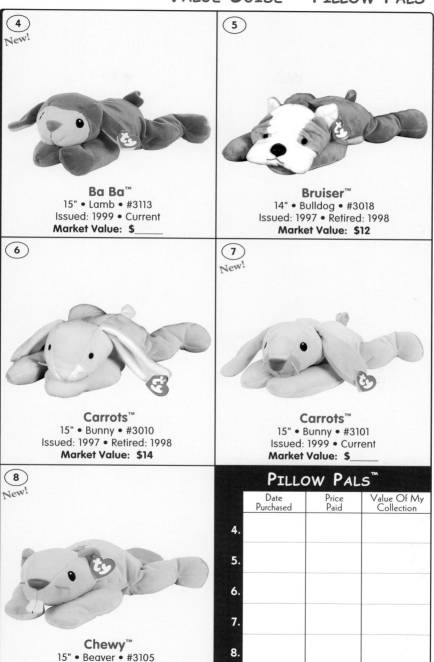

(4) New!

Ba Ba™
15" • Lamb • #3113
Issued: 1999 • Current
Market Value: $_____

(5)

Bruiser™
14" • Bulldog • #3018
Issued: 1997 • Retired: 1998
Market Value: $12

(6)

Carrots™
15" • Bunny • #3010
Issued: 1997 • Retired: 1998
Market Value: $14

(7) New!

Carrots™
15" • Bunny • #3101
Issued: 1999 • Current
Market Value: $_____

(8) New!

Chewy™
15" • Beaver • #3105
Issued: 1999 • Current
Market Value: $_____

PILLOW PALS™

	Date Purchased	Price Paid	Value Of My Collection
4.			
5.			
6.			
7.			
8.			
PENCIL TOTALS			

PILLOW PALS™

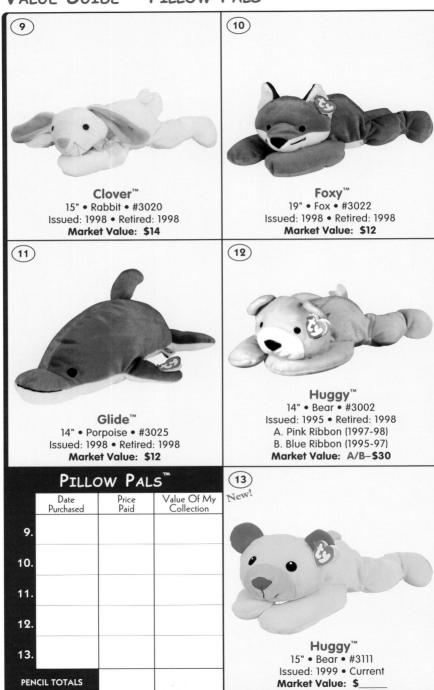

9

Clover™
15" • Rabbit • #3020
Issued: 1998 • Retired: 1998
Market Value: $14

10

Foxy™
19" • Fox • #3022
Issued: 1998 • Retired: 1998
Market Value: $12

11

Glide™
14" • Porpoise • #3025
Issued: 1998 • Retired: 1998
Market Value: $12

12

Huggy™
14" • Bear • #3002
Issued: 1995 • Retired: 1998
A. Pink Ribbon (1997-98)
B. Blue Ribbon (1995-97)
Market Value: A/B–$30

Pillow Pals™

	Date Purchased	Price Paid	Value Of My Collection
9.			
10.			
11.			
12.			
13.			
PENCIL TOTALS			

13 New!

Huggy™
15" • Bear • #3111
Issued: 1999 • Current
Market Value: $_____

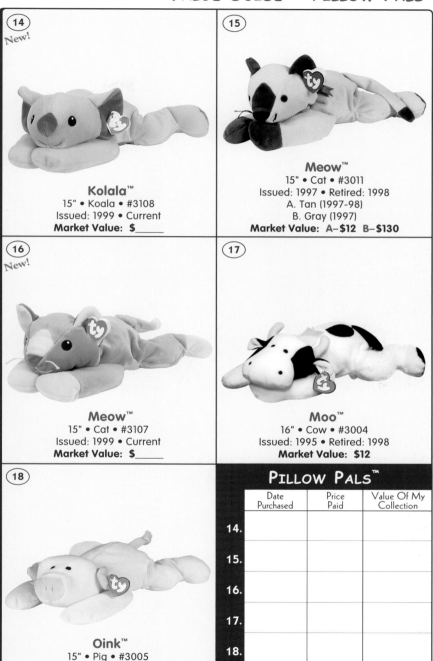

(14)
New!

Kolala™
15" • Koala • #3108
Issued: 1999 • Current
Market Value: $_____

(15)

Meow™
15" • Cat • #3011
Issued: 1997 • Retired: 1998
A. Tan (1997-98)
B. Gray (1997)
Market Value: A–$12 B–$130

(16)
New!

Meow™
15" • Cat • #3107
Issued: 1999 • Current
Market Value: $_____

(17)

Moo™
16" • Cow • #3004
Issued: 1995 • Retired: 1998
Market Value: $12

(18)

Oink™
15" • Pig • #3005
Issued: 1995 • Retired: 1998
Market Value: $14

PILLOW PALS™

	Date Purchased	Price Paid	Value Of My Collection
14.			
15.			
16.			
17.			
18.			
PENCIL TOTALS			

PILLOW PALS™

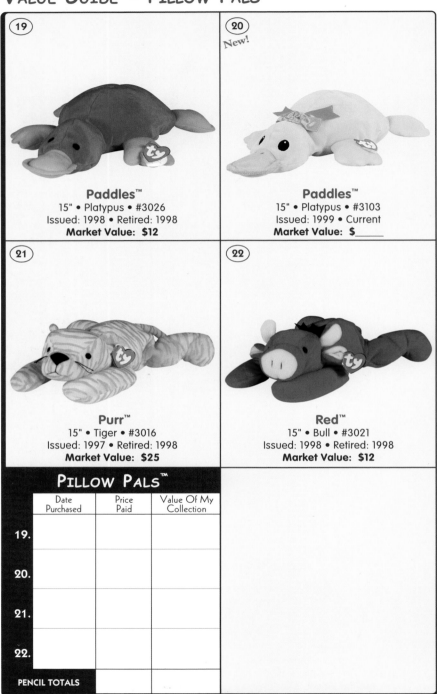

(19)

Paddles™
15" • Platypus • #3026
Issued: 1998 • Retired: 1998
Market Value: $12

(20) *New!*

Paddles™
15" • Platypus • #3103
Issued: 1999 • Current
Market Value: $_____

(21)

Purr™
15" • Tiger • #3016
Issued: 1997 • Retired: 1998
Market Value: $25

(22)

Red™
15" • Bull • #3021
Issued: 1998 • Retired: 1998
Market Value: $12

PILLOW PALS™

	Date Purchased	Price Paid	Value Of My Collection
19.			
20.			
21.			
22.			
PENCIL TOTALS			

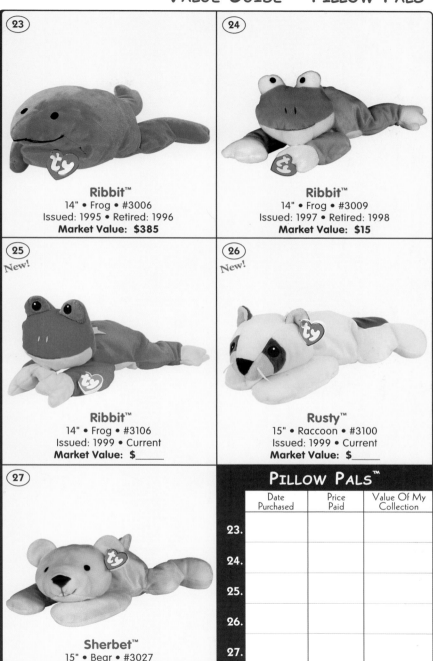

(23)

Ribbit™
14" • Frog • #3006
Issued: 1995 • Retired: 1996
Market Value: $385

(24)

Ribbit™
14" • Frog • #3009
Issued: 1997 • Retired: 1998
Market Value: $15

(25) New!

Ribbit™
14" • Frog • #3106
Issued: 1999 • Current
Market Value: $_____

(26) New!

Rusty™
15" • Raccoon • #3100
Issued: 1999 • Current
Market Value: $_____

(27)

Sherbet™
15" • Bear • #3027
Issued: 1998 • Retired: 1998
Market Value: $18

PILLOW PALS™

	Date Purchased	Price Paid	Value Of My Collection
23.			
24.			
25.			
26.			
27.			
PENCIL TOTALS			

PILLOW PALS™

127

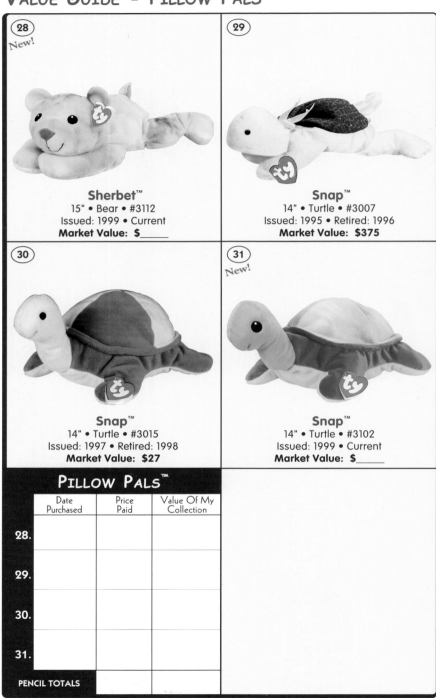

28 New!

Sherbet™
15" • Bear • #3112
Issued: 1999 • Current
Market Value: $_____

29

Snap™
14" • Turtle • #3007
Issued: 1995 • Retired: 1996
Market Value: $375

30

Snap™
14" • Turtle • #3015
Issued: 1997 • Retired: 1998
Market Value: $27

31 New!

Snap™
14" • Turtle • #3102
Issued: 1999 • Current
Market Value: $_____

PILLOW PALS™

	Date Purchased	Price Paid	Value Of My Collection
28.			
29.			
30.			
31.			
PENCIL TOTALS			

(32)

Snuggy™
14" • Bear • #3001
Issued: 1995 • Retired: 1998
A. Blue Ribbon (1997-98)
B. Pink Ribbon (1995-97)
Market Value: A/B–$30

(33)

Speckles™
15" • Leopard • #3017
Issued: 1997 • Retired: 1998
Market Value: $12

(34)

Spotty™
15" • Dalmatian • #3019
Issued: 1998 • Retired: 1998
Market Value: $12

(35)

Squirt™
15" • Elephant • #3013
Issued: 1997 • Retired: 1998
Market Value: $12

(36)
New!

Squirt™
15" • Elephant • #3109
Issued: 1999 • Current
Market Value: $_____

PILLOW PALS™

	Date Purchased	Price Paid	Value Of My Collection
32.			
33.			
34.			
35.			
36.			
PENCIL TOTALS			

PILLOW PALS™

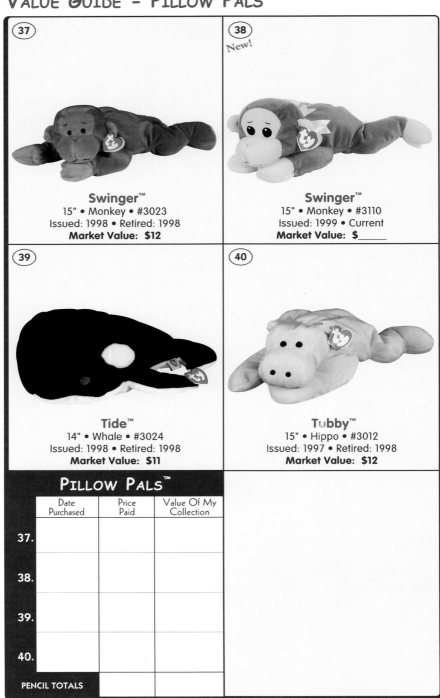

(37)

Swinger™
15" • Monkey • #3023
Issued: 1998 • Retired: 1998
Market Value: $12

(38)

New!

Swinger™
15" • Monkey • #3110
Issued: 1999 • Current
Market Value: $_____

(39)

Tide™
14" • Whale • #3024
Issued: 1998 • Retired: 1998
Market Value: $11

(40)

Tubby™
15" • Hippo • #3012
Issued: 1997 • Retired: 1998
Market Value: $12

PILLOW PALS™

	Date Purchased	Price Paid	Value Of My Collection
37.			
38.			
39.			
40.			
PENCIL TOTALS			

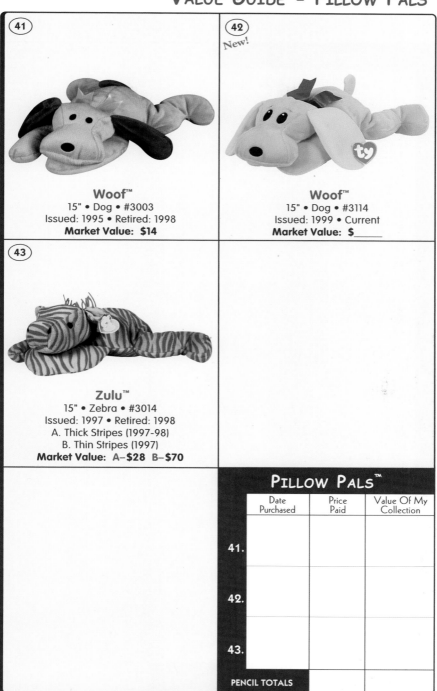

(41)

Woof™
15" • Dog • #3003
Issued: 1995 • Retired: 1998
Market Value: $14

(42)

New!

Woof™
15" • Dog • #3114
Issued: 1999 • Current
Market Value: $_____

(43)

Zulu™
15" • Zebra • #3014
Issued: 1997 • Retired: 1998
A. Thick Stripes (1997-98)
B. Thin Stripes (1997)
Market Value: A–$28 B–$70

PILLOW PALS™

	Date Purchased	Price Paid	Value Of My Collection
41.			
42.			
43.			
PENCIL TOTALS			

PILLOW PALS™

VALUE GUIDE - FUTURE RELEASES

Use these pages to record future Pillow Pals™ releases.

PILLOW PALS™	Date Purchased	Price Paid	Value Of My Collection
	PENCIL TOTALS		

A MENAGERIE OF PLUSH

Originally introduced in 1986 as a small litter of cats and dogs, the *Ty Plush* collection now includes 358 animals from all walks of life. This branch of the Ty family tree is divided into the following five categories and are listed separately in the value guide: bears, cats, dogs, country and wildlife. Unfortunately, many of these creatures are no longer available. "Baby Patches" (a dog) is the only new piece for Spring 1999 and this season, many of the old, familiar critters have slipped quietly into retirement.

BEARS

Although they did not join the collection until 1988, the bears now total 133 pieces and have become the largest category within *Ty Plush*. However, only 14 of the bruins are still available, including three which have donned sweaters and joined *The Attic Treasures Collection*.

1991 Ty Collectable Bear™
21" • Bear • #5500
Issued: 1991 • Retired: 1991
Market Value: $1,200

1992 Ty Collectable Bear™
21" • Bear • #5500
Issued: 1992 • Retired: 1992
A. "1992 Ty Collectable Bear™" Version
B. "Edmond™" Version
Market Value: A–$630 B–$240

BEARS

	Date Purchased	Price Paid	Value Of My Collection
1.			
2.			
PENCIL TOTALS			

BEARS

(3)

1997 Holiday Bear™
14" • Bear • #5700
Issued: 1997 • Retired: 1997
Market Value: $50

(4)

Aurora™
13" • Polar Bear • #5103
Issued: 1996 • Retired: 1997
Market Value: $48

(5)

Baby Buddy™
20" • Bear • #5011
Issued: 1992 • Retired: 1992
Market Value: $480

(6)

Baby Cinnamon™
13" • Bear • #5105
Issued: 1996 • Retired: 1996
Market Value: $45

BEARS

	Date Purchased	Price Paid	Value Of My Collection
3.			
4.			
5.			
6.			
7.			
PENCIL TOTALS			

(7)

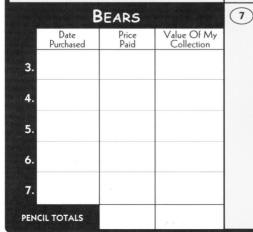

Baby Curly™
12" • Bear • #5017
Issued: 1993 • Retired: 1997
Market Value: $40

8

Baby Curly™
(moved to Attic Treasures™ in 1999)
12" • Bear • #5018
Issued: 1993 • Current
A. Sweater (1998-Current)
B. Ribbon (1993-98)
Market Value: A–$_____ B–N/E

9

Baby Ginger™
14" • Bear • #5108
Issued: 1997 • Retired: 1998
Market Value: $18

10

Baby Paws™
12" • Bear • #5110
Issued: 1997 • Current
Market Value: $_____

11

Baby Paws™
12" • Bear • #5111
Issued: 1997 • Current
Market Value: $_____

12

Baby Paws™
12" • Bear • #5112
Issued: 1998 • Retired: 1998
Market Value: $20

BEARS

	Date Purchased	Price Paid	Value Of My Collection
8.			
9.			
10.			
11.			
12.			
PENCIL TOTALS			

BEARS

(13)

Baby PJ™
12" • Bear • #5016
Issued: 1993 • Retired: 1998
Market Value: $22

(14)

Baby PJ™
12" • Bear • #5100
Issued: 1994 • Retired: 1994
Market Value: $80

(15)

Baby Powder™
14" • Bear • #5109
Issued: 1997 • Retired: 1998
Market Value: $18

(16)

Baby Spice™
13" • Bear • #5104
Issued: 1996 • Retired: 1997
A. "Baby Spice™" Swing Tag
B. "ByBy Spice™" Swing Tag
Market Value: A/B–$35

BEARS

	Date Purchased	Price Paid	Value Of My Collection
13.			
14.			
15.			
16.			
17.			
PENCIL TOTALS			

(17)

Bailey™
19" • Bear • #5502
Issued: 1997 • Retired: 1997
Market Value: $45

(18)

Bamboo™
13" • Panda • #5106
Issued: 1996 • Retired: 1997
Market Value: $42

(19)

Bamboo™
12" • Panda • #5113
Issued: 1998 • Retired: 1998
Market Value: $15

(20)

Baron™
18" • Bear • #5200
Issued: 1995 • Retired: 1995
Market Value: $105

(21)

Beanie Bear™
12" • Bear • #5000
Issued: 1988 • Retired: 1990
Market Value: $815

(22)

Beanie Bear™
12" • Bear • #5100
Issued: 1991 • Retired: 1992
Market Value: $800

BEARS

	Date Purchased	Price Paid	Value Of My Collection
18.			
19.			
20.			
21.			
22.			
PENCIL TOTALS			

BEARS

(23)

Beanie Bear™
12" • Bear • #5101
Issued: 1991 • Retired: 1991
Market Value: N/E

(24)

Beanie Bear™
12" • Bear • #5102
Issued: 1991 • Retired: 1991
Market Value: N/E

(25)

Big Beanie Bear™
15" • Bear • #5011
Issued: 1990 • Retired: 1990
Market Value: $850

(26)

Big Beanie Bear™
15" • Bear • #5200
Issued: 1991 • Retired: 1991
Market Value: $800

BEARS

	Date Purchased	Price Paid	Value Of My Collection
23.			
24.			
25.			
26.			
27.			
PENCIL TOTALS			

(27)

Big Beanie Bear™
15" • Bear • #5201
Issued: 1991 • Retired: 1991
Market Value: N/E

(28)

Big Beanie Bear™
15" • Bear • #5202
Issued: 1991 • Retired: 1991
Market Value: $850

(29)

Big Pudgy™
28" • Bear • #9006
Issued: 1994 • Retired: 1996
Market Value: $230

(30)

Big Shaggy™
26" • Bear • #9015
Issued: 1992 • Retired: 1992
Market Value: $315

(31)

Blackie™
13" • Bear • #5003
Issued: 1988 • Retired: 1990
Market Value: $550

(32)

Brownie™
13" • Bear • #5100
Issued: 1996 • Retired: 1996
Market Value: $62

BEARS

	Date Purchased	Price Paid	Value Of My Collection
28.			
29.			
30.			
31.			
32.			
PENCIL TOTALS			

BEARS

(33)

Buddy™
20" • Bear • #5007
Issued: 1990 • Retired: 1992
Market Value: $525

(34)

Buddy™
20" • Bear • #5019
Issued: 1993 • Retired: 1996
Market Value: $55

(35)

Cinnamon™
13" • Bear • #5004
Issued: 1989 • Retired: 1990
Market Value: $745

(36)

Cinnamon™
18" • Bear • #5021
Issued: 1996 • Retired: 1996
Market Value: $55

BEARS

	Date Purchased	Price Paid	Value Of My Collection
33.			
34.			
35.			
36.			
37.			
PENCIL TOTALS			

(37)

Cocoa™
12" • Bear • #5107
Issued: 1997 • Retired: 1998
Market Value: $15

(38)

Curly™
18" • Bear • #5300
Issued: 1991 • Retired: 1997
A. 18" (1993-97)
B. 22" (1991-92)
Market Value: A/B–$50

(39)

Curly™
22" • Bear • #5301
Issued: 1991 • Retired: 1991
Market Value: N/E

(40)

Curly™
(moved to Attic Treasures™ in 1999)
18" • Bear • #5302
Issued: 1991 • Current
A. 18"/Sweater (1998-Current)
B. 18"/Ribbon (1993-98)
C. 22"/Ribbon (1991-92)
Market Value: A–$_____ B–N/E C–N/E

(41)

Cuzzy™
13" • Bear • #5203
Issued: 1996 • Retired: 1997
Market Value: $85

BEARS

	Date Purchased	Price Paid	Value Of My Collection
38.			
39.			
40.			
41.			
PENCIL TOTALS			

BEARS

VALUE GUIDE - TY® PLUSH

(42)

Dumpling™
12" • Bear • #5022
Issued: 1996 • Retired: 1996
Market Value: $65

(43)

Dumpling™
12" • Bear • #5023
Issued: 1996 • Retired: 1996
Market Value: $65

(44)

Eleanor™
19" • Bear • #5500
Issued: 1996 • Retired: 1997
Market Value: $55

(45)

Faith™
10" • Bear • #5600
Issued: 1996 • Current
Market Value: $____

BEARS

	Date Purchased	Price Paid	Value Of My Collection
42.			
43.			
44.			
45.			
46.			
PENCIL TOTALS			

(46)

Forest™
12" • Bear • #5114
Issued: 1998 • Retired: 1998
Market Value: $15

47

Fuzzy™
13" • Bear • #5204
Issued: 1996 • Retired: 1997
Market Value: $82

48

Ginger™
18" • Bear • #5306
Issued: 1997 • Retired: 1997
Market Value: $45

49

Honey™
14" • Bear • #5004
Issued: 1991 • Retired: 1994
A. Blue Ribbon (1992-94)
B. Red Ribbon (1991)
Market Value: A/B–$200

50

Hope™
10" • Bear • #5601
Issued: 1996 • Retired: 1998
Market Value: $23

51

Jumbo PJ™
40" • Bear • #9016
Issued: 1994 • Retired: 1994
Market Value: N/E

BEARS

	Date Purchased	Price Paid	Value Of My Collection
47.			
48.			
49.			
50.			
51.			
PENCIL TOTALS			

BEARS

143

(52)

Jumbo PJ™
40" • Bear • #9020
Issued: 1992 • Retired: 1998
Market Value: $120

(53)

Jumbo Pumpkin™
40" • Bear • #9017
Issued: 1995 • Retired: 1996
Market Value: $600

(54)

Jumbo Rumples™
40" • Bear • #9016
Issued: 1995 • Retired: 1996
Market Value: $210

(55)

Jumbo Shaggy™
40" • Bear • #9016
Issued: 1992 • Retired: 1993
Market Value: $450

BEARS

	Date Purchased	Price Paid	Value Of My Collection
52.			
53.			
54.			
55.			
56.			
PENCIL TOTALS			

(56)

Jumbo Shaggy™
40" • Bear • #9017
Issued: 1992 • Retired: 1994
Market Value: $450

57

Jumbo Shaggy™
40" • Bear • #9026
Issued: 1993 • Retired: 1996
Market Value: $450

58

Kasey™
20" • Koala • #5006
Issued: 1989 • Retired: 1991
A. 20"/Gray (1990-91)
B. 13"/Brown (1989)
Market Value: A–$725 B–$825

59

Large Curly™
26" • Bear • #9018
Issued: 1992 • Retired: 1997
Market Value: $85

60

Large Curly™
(moved to Attic Treasures™ in 1999)
26" • Bear • #9019
Issued: 1992 • Current
A. Sweater (1998-Current)
B. Ribbon (1992-98)
Market Value: A–$_____ B–N/E

61

Large Ginger™
22" • Bear • #9027
Issued: 1997 • Retired: 1997
Market Value: $70

BEARS

	Date Purchased	Price Paid	Value Of My Collection
57.			
58.			
59.			
60.			
61.			
PENCIL TOTALS			

BEARS

(62)

Large Honey™
26" • Bear • #9021
Issued: 1992 • Retired: 1994
Market Value: $280

(63)

Large McGee™
26" • Bear • #9005
Issued: 1992 • Retired: 1997
Market Value: $80

(64)

Large Moonbeam™
20" • Bear • #9009
Issued: 1995 • Retired: 1995
Market Value: $195

(65)

Large Paws™
28" • Bear • #9029
Issued: 1997 • Current
Market Value: $_____

Bears

	Date Purchased	Price Paid	Value Of My Collection
62.			
63.			
64.			
65.			
66.			
PENCIL TOTALS			

(66)

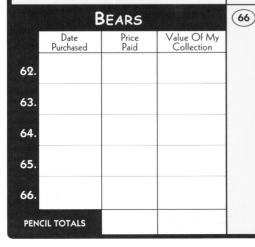

Large Paws™
28" • Bear • #9030
Issued: 1997 • Current
Market Value: $_____

(67)

Large Paws™
28" • Bear • #9031
Issued: 1998 • Current
Market Value: $_____

(68)

Large Ping Pong™
26" • Panda • #9010
Issued: 1992 • Retired: 1993
Market Value: $600

(69)

Large PJ™
26" • Bear • #9012
Issued: 1992 • Retired: 1998
A. 26" (1993-98)
B. 24" (1992)
Market Value: A–$48 B–N/E

(70)

Large PJ™
26" • Bear • #9014
Issued: 1994 • Retired: 1994
Market Value: $180

(71)

Large Powder™
22" • Bear • #9028
Issued: 1997 • Retired: 1997
Market Value: $85

BEARS

	Date Purchased	Price Paid	Value Of My Collection
67.			
68.			
69.			
70.			
71.			
PENCIL TOTALS			

BEARS

(72)

Large Pumpkin™
26" • Bear • #9015
Issued: 1995 • Retired: 1996
Market Value: $190

(73)

Large Rumples™
26" • Bear • #9000
Issued: 1995 • Retired: 1995
Market Value: $190

(74)

Large Rumples™
26" • Bear • #9002
Issued: 1995 • Retired: 1996
Market Value: $120

(75)

Large Scruffy™
28" • Bear • #9000
Issued: 1992 • Retired: 1993
Market Value: $225

BEARS

	Date Purchased	Price Paid	Value Of My Collection
72.			
73.			
74.			
75.			
76.			
PENCIL TOTALS			

(76)

Large Scruffy™
28" • Bear • #9013
Issued: 1992 • Retired: 1992
Market Value: $340

(77)

Large Shaggy™
26" • Bear • #9014
Issued: 1992 • Retired: 1993
Market Value: $310

(78)

Large Shaggy™
26" • Bear • #9015
Issued: 1993 • Retired: 1994
Market Value: $310

(79)

Large Shaggy™
26" • Bear • #9025
Issued: 1993 • Retired: 1996
Market Value: $180

(80)

Large Snowball™
26" • Bear • #9009
Issued: 1992 • Retired: 1993
Market Value: $260

(81)

Lazy™
20" • Bear • #5008
Issued: 1995 • Retired: 1996
Market Value: $65

BEARS

	Date Purchased	Price Paid	Value Of My Collection
77.			
78.			
79.			
80.			
81.			
PENCIL TOTALS			

BEARS

Value Guide - Ty® Plush

82

Magee™
10" • Bear • #5027
Issued: 1998 • Current
Market Value: $_____

83

Mandarin™
13" • Panda • #5201
Issued: 1996 • Retired: 1997
Market Value: $93

84

McGee™
14" • Bear • #5001
Issued: 1988 • Retired: 1997
A. 14" (1991-97)
B. 13" (1988-90)
Market Value: A–$65 B–$750

85

Midnight™
20" • Bear • #5009
Issued: 1990 • Retired: 1993
A. Black & Brown (1991, 1993)
B. All Black (1990)
Market Value: A/B–$370

BEARS

	Date Purchased	Price Paid	Value Of My Collection
82.			
83.			
84.			
85.			
86.			
PENCIL TOTALS			

86

Midnight™
13" • Bear • #5101
Issued: 1996 • Retired: 1996
Market Value: $65

150

(87)

Moonbeam™
14" • Bear • #5009
Issued: 1995 • Retired: 1995
Market Value: $165

(88)

Nutmeg™
18" • Bear • #5013
Issued: 1996 • Retired: 1997
Market Value: $60

(89)

Oreo™
20" • Panda • #5005
Issued: 1994 • Retired: 1996
Market Value: $85

(90)

Oreo™
20" • Panda • #5010
Issued: 1990 • Retired: 1991
Market Value: $320

(91)

Papa PJ™
50" • Bear • #9021
Issued: 1997 • Retired: 1998
Market Value: $225

BEARS

	Date Purchased	Price Paid	Value Of My Collection
87.			
88.			
89.			
90.			
91.			
PENCIL TOTALS			

BEARS

(92)

Papa Pumpkin™
50" • Bear • #9023
Issued: 1995 • Retired: 1996
Market Value: $1,400

(93)

Papa Rumples™
50" • Bear • #9022
Issued: 1995 • Retired: 1996
Market Value: $1,000

(94)

Papa Shaggy™
50" • Bear • #9024
Issued: 1994 • Retired: 1996
Market Value: $1,450

(95)

Paws™
18" • Bear • #5024
Issued: 1997 • Current
Market Value: $_____

BEARS

	Date Purchased	Price Paid	Value Of My Collection
92.			
93.			
94.			
95.			
96.			
PENCIL TOTALS			

(96)

Paws™
18" • Bear • #5025
Issued: 1997 • Current
Market Value: $_____

(97)

Paws™
18" • Bear • #5026
Issued: 1998 • Current
Market Value: $_____

(98)

Ping Pong™
14" • Panda • #5005
Issued: 1989 • Retired: 1993
A. 14" (1991-93)
B. 13" (1989-90)
Market Value: A–$330 B–$650

(99)

Ping Pong™
N/A • Panda • #5007
Issued: 1989 • Retired: 1989
Market Value: N/E

(100)

PJ™
18" • Bear • #5200
Issued: 1994 • Retired: 1994
Market Value: $145

(101)

PJ™
18" • Bear • #5400
Issued: 1991 • Retired: 1998
A. 18" (1993-98)
B. 22" (1991-92)
Market Value: A–$32 B–N/E

BEARS

	Date Purchased	Price Paid	Value Of My Collection
97.			
98.			
99.			
100.			
101.			
PENCIL TOTALS			

BEARS

(102)

Powder™
18" • Bear • #5307
Issued: 1997 • Retired: 1997
Market Value: $65

(103)

Prayer Bear™
14" • Bear • #5600
Issued: 1992 • Retired: 1994
Market Value: $240

(104)

Prayer Bear™
14" • Bear • #5601
Issued: 1992 • Retired: 1993
Market Value: $290

(105)

Pudgy™
14" • Bear • #5006
Issued: 1994 • Retired: 1996
Market Value: $135

BEARS

	Date Purchased	Price Paid	Value Of My Collection
102.			
103.			
104.			
105.			
106.			
PENCIL TOTALS			

(106)

Pumpkin™
18" • Bear • #5304
Issued: 1995 • Retired: 1996
Market Value: $155

(107)

Rags™
12" • Bear • #5102
Issued: 1992 • Retired: 1996
Market Value: $70

(108)

Romeo™
14" • Bear • #5310
Issued: 1998 • Current
A. Gold Ribbon/I Love You (1998-Current)
B. Purple Ribbon/Mother's Day (1998)
C. Red Ribbon (1998)
Market Value: A-$_____ B-$30 C-N/E

(109)

Ruffles™
12" • Bear • #5014
Issued: 1995 • Retired: 1995
Market Value: $110

(110)

Rufus™
18" • Bear • #5015
Issued: 1993 • Retired: 1997
Market Value: $55

(111)

Rumples™
18" • Bear • #5002
Issued: 1995 • Retired: 1996
Market Value: $75

BEARS

	Date Purchased	Price Paid	Value Of My Collection
107.			
108.			
109.			
110.			
111.			
PENCIL TOTALS			

BEARS

112

Rumples™
18" • Bear • #5003
Issued: 1995 • Retired: 1995
A. Brown Nose/Green Ribbon (1995)
B. Pink Nose/Pink Ribbon (1995)
Market Value: A/B–$100

113

Sam™
18" • Bear • #5010
Issued: 1995 • Retired: 1996
Market Value: $225

114

Scruffy™
18" • Bear • #5012
Issued: 1991 • Retired: 1994
Market Value: $150

115

Scruffy™
18" • Bear • #5013
Issued: 1992 • Retired: 1995
A. Gold (1995)
B. Cream (1992)
Market Value: A–N/E B–$230

BEARS

	Date Purchased	Price Paid	Value Of My Collection
112.			
113.			
114.			
115.			
116.			
PENCIL TOTALS			

116

Shadow™
20" • Bear • #5011
Issued: 1994 • Retired: 1996
Market Value: $80

117

Shaggy™
18" • Bear • #5303
Issued: 1992 • Retired: 1993
A. 18" (1993)
B. 24" (1992)
Market Value: A/B–$200

118

Shaggy™
18" • Bear • #5304
Issued: 1992 • Retired: 1994
Market Value: $200

119

Shaggy™
18" • Bear • #5305
Issued: 1993 • Retired: 1996
Market Value: $105

120

Snowball™
14" • Bear • #5002
Issued: 1988 • Retired: 1993
A. 14"/Red Ribbon (1991-93)
B. 13"/Red Ribbon (1990)
C. 13"/Blue Ribbon (1989)
D. 13"/No Ribbon (1988)
Market Value: A/B/C/D–N/E

BEARS

	Date Purchased	Price Paid	Value Of My Collection
117.			
118.			
119.			
120.			
PENCIL TOTALS			

BEARS

(121)

Spice™
18" • Bear • #5020
Issued: 1996 • Retired: 1997
Market Value: $45

(122)

Sugar™
14" • Bear • #5007
Issued: 1995 • Retired: 1995
Market Value: $100

(123)

Sugar™
14" • Polar Bear • #5008
Issued: 1990 • Retired: 1991
A. 14" (1991)
B. 20" (1990)
Market Value: A/B–$205

(124)

Super Buddy™
32" • Bear • #9006
Issued: 1990 • Retired: 1991
Market Value: N/E

BEARS

	Date Purchased	Price Paid	Value Of My Collection
121.			
122.			
123.			
124.			
125.			
PENCIL TOTALS			

(125)

Super McGee™
26" • Bear • #9005
Issued: 1991 • Retired: 1991
Market Value: N/E

126

Super Ping Pong™
26" • Panda • #9010
Issued: 1991 • Retired: 1991
Market Value: N/E

127

Super PJ™
24" • Bear • #9012
Issued: 1991 • Retired: 1991
Market Value: N/E

128

Super Scruffy™
28" • Bear • #9000
Issued: 1991 • Retired: 1991
Market Value: $400

129

Super Snowball™
26" • Bear • #9009
Issued: 1991 • Retired: 1991
Market Value: N/E

130

Theodore™
19" • Bear • #5501
Issued: 1996 • Retired: 1997
Market Value: $65

BEARS

	Date Purchased	Price Paid	Value Of My Collection
126.			
127.			
128.			
129.			
130.			
PENCIL TOTALS			

BEARS

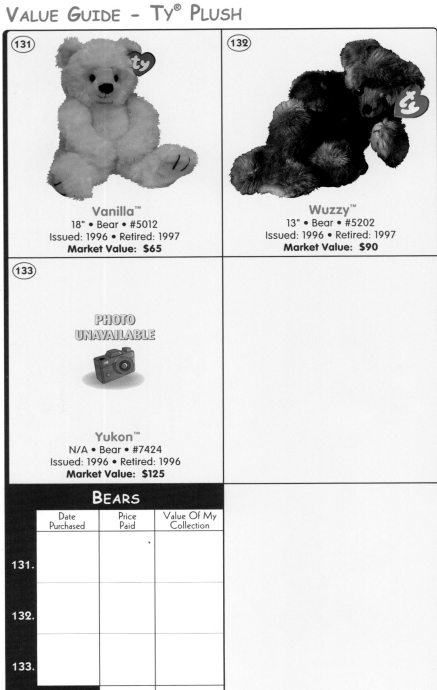

(131)

Vanilla™
18" • Bear • #5012
Issued: 1996 • Retired: 1997
Market Value: $65

(132)

Wuzzy™
13" • Bear • #5202
Issued: 1996 • Retired: 1997
Market Value: $90

(133)

PHOTO
UNAVAILABLE

Yukon™
N/A • Bear • #7424
Issued: 1996 • Retired: 1996
Market Value: $125

BEARS

	Date Purchased	Price Paid	Value Of My Collection
131.			
132.			
133.			
PENCIL TOTALS			

CATS

A total of 47 cats have clawed their way into the *Ty Plush* collection since it debuted in 1986. The four legged felines make "purr-fect" companions, if you can find them. Only four of the pieces are still available!

(134)

Al E. Kat™
22" • Cat • #1111
Issued: 1988 • Current
A. 22"/Curled (1996-Current)
B. 20"/Curled (1992-95)
C. 20"/Flat (1989-91)
D. 23"/Flat (1988)
**Market Value: A-$_____ B-N/E
C-$110 D-$750**

(135)

Al E. Kat™
22" • Cat • #1112
Issued: 1989 • Retired: 1998
A. 22"/Curled (1996-98)
B. 20"/Curled (1992-95)
C. 20"/Flat (1989-91)
Market Value: A-$24 B-N/E C-$110

(136)

Angel™
20" • Persian • #1001
Issued: 1988 • Retired: 1995
Market Value: $80

(137)

Angel™
20" • Himalayan • #1001H
Issued: 1988 • Retired: 1990
Market Value: N/E

CATS

	Date Purchased	Price Paid	Value Of My Collection
134.			
135.			
136.			
137.			
PENCIL TOTALS			

CATS

(138)

Angel™
17" • Persian • #1122
Issued: 1998 • Retired: 1998
Market Value: $22

(139)

Angora™
N/A • Cat • #1001
Issued: 1986 • Retired: 1986
Market Value: N/E

(140)

Baby Angora™
N/A • Cat • #1002
Issued: 1986 • Retired: 1986
Market Value: N/E

(141)

Baby Bijan™
N/A • Cat • #1006
Issued: 1986 • Retired: 1986
Market Value: N/E

CATS

	Date Purchased	Price Paid	Value Of My Collection
138.			
139.			
140.			
141.			
142.			
PENCIL TOTALS			

(142)

Baby Butterball™
N/A • Cat • #2006
Issued: 1986 • Retired: 1986
Market Value: N/E

(143)

Baby Jasmine™
N/A • Cat • #1004
Issued: 1986 • Retired: 1986
Market Value: N/E

(144)

Baby Kasha™
N/A • Cat • #1008
Issued: 1986 • Retired: 1986
Market Value: N/E

(145)

Baby Kimchi™
N/A • Cat • #2004
Issued: 1986 • Retired: 1986
Market Value: N/E

(146)

Baby Oscar™
N/A • Cat • #2008
Issued: 1986 • Retired: 1986
Market Value: N/E

(147)

Baby Snowball™
N/A • Cat • #2002
Issued: 1986 • Retired: 1986
Market Value: N/E

CATS

	Date Purchased	Price Paid	Value Of My Collection
143.			
144.			
145.			
146.			
147.			
PENCIL TOTALS			

CATS

(148)

Bijan™
N/A • Cat • #1005
Issued: 1986 • Retired: 1986
Market Value: N/E

(149)

Boots™
16" • Cat • #1123
Issued: 1998 • Current
Market Value: $_____

(150)

PHOTO
UNAVAILABLE

Butterball™
N/A • Cat • #2005
Issued: 1986 • Retired: 1986
Market Value: N/E

(151)

Coal™
16" • Cat • #1119
Issued: 1997 • Retired: 1997
Market Value: $45

CATS

	Date Purchased	Price Paid	Value Of My Collection
148.			
149.			
150.			
151.			
152.			
PENCIL TOTALS			

(152)

Crystal™
16" • Cat • #1120
Issued: 1997 • Current
Market Value: $_____

(153)

Fluffy™
15" • Persian • #1002
Issued: 1996 • Retired: 1997
Market Value: $45

(154)

Frisky™
17" • Cat • #1007
Issued: 1996 • Retired: 1997
Market Value: $88

(155)

Ginger™
20" • Cat • #1007
Issued: 1988 • Retired: 1990
Market Value: $425

(156)

Ginger™
20" • Himalayan • #1007H
Issued: 1988 • Retired: 1990
Market Value: N/E

(157)

Jasmine™
N/A • Cat • #1003
Issued: 1986 • Retired: 1986
Market Value: N/E

CATS

	Date Purchased	Price Paid	Value Of My Collection
153.			
154.			
155.			
156.			
157.			
PENCIL TOTALS			

CATS

(158)

Kasha™
N/A • Cat • #1007
Issued: 1986 • Retired: 1986
Market Value: N/E

(159)

Kimchi™
N/A • Cat • #2003
Issued: 1986 • Retired: 1986
Market Value: N/E

(160)

Licorice™
20" • Persian • #1009
Issued: 1988 • Retired: 1995
Market Value: $100

(161)

Licorice™
17" • Persian • #1125
Issued: 1998 • Retired: 1998
Market Value: $17

CATS

	Date Purchased	Price Paid	Value Of My Collection
158.			
159.			
160.			
161.			
162.			
PENCIL TOTALS			

(162)

Maggie™
22" • Cat • #1115
Issued: 1992 • Retired: 1998
A. 22"/Curled (1996-98)
B. 20"/Flat (1992-95)
Market Value: A–$25 B–$90

(163)

Mittens™
12" • Cat • #1117
Issued: 1993 • Retired: 1994
Market Value: $210

(164)

Mittens™
12" • Cat • #1118
Issued: 1993 • Retired: 1994
Market Value: $210

(165)

PHOTO UNAVAILABLE

Oscar™
N/A • Cat • #2007
Issued: 1986 • Retired: 1986
Market Value: N/E

(166)

Patches™
20" • Cat • #1114
Issued: 1991 • Retired: 1995
Market Value: $155

CATS

	Date Purchased	Price Paid	Value Of My Collection
163.			
164.			
165.			
166.			
PENCIL TOTALS			

CATS

(167)

Peaches™
20" • Cat • #1003
Issued: 1988 • Retired: 1993
Market Value: $420

(168)

Peaches™
20" • Himalayan • #1003H
Issued: 1988 • Retired: 1990
Market Value: N/E

(169)

Puffy™
15" • Persian • #1003
Issued: 1996 • Retired: 1997
Market Value: $45

(170)

Scratch™
15" • Cat • #1117
Issued: 1996 • Retired: 1997
Market Value: $85

CATS

	Date Purchased	Price Paid	Value Of My Collection
167.			
168.			
169.			
170.			
171.			
PENCIL TOTALS			

(171)

Screech™
15" • Cat • #1116
Issued: 1995 • Retired: 1996
A. Collar (1996)
B. No Collar (1995)
Market Value: A/B–$100

(172)

Shadow™
20" • Cat • #1112
Issued: 1988 • Retired: 1988
Market Value: $850

(173)

Sherlock™
20" • Cat • #1110
Issued: 1990 • Retired: 1992
Market Value: $470

(174)

Silky™
15" • Persian • #1004
Issued: 1996 • Retired: 1997
Market Value: $45

(175)

Smokey™
20" • Cat • #1005
Issued: 1988 • Retired: 1993
Market Value: $320

(176)

Smokey™
20" • Himalayan • #1005H
Issued: 1988 • Retired: 1990
Market Value: N/E

CATS

	Date Purchased	Price Paid	Value Of My Collection
172.			
173.			
174.			
175.			
176.			
PENCIL TOTALS			

CATS

177

PHOTO UNAVAILABLE

Snowball™
N/A • Cat • #2001
Issued: 1986 • Retired: 1986
Market Value: N/E

178

Socks™
12" • Cat • #1116
Issued: 1993 • Retired: 1994
Market Value: $195

179

Spice™
17" • Cat • #1121
Issued: 1998 • Current
Market Value: $_____

180

Tumbles™
17" • Cat • #1008
Issued: 1996 • Retired: 1997
Market Value: $100

CATS

	Date Purchased	Price Paid	Value Of My Collection
177.			
178.			
179.			
180.			
PENCIL TOTALS			

DOGS

Dog lovers will adore this collection of 57 pooches which features every kind of canine, from the well-groomed "Yorkie" the Yorkshire terrier to "Large Rusty" the mutt. A new addition to the dog family for Spring 1999 is the adorable "Baby Patches."

(181)

Ace™
12" • Dalmatian • #2027
Issued: 1998 • Retired: 1998
Market Value: $15

(182)

Ashes™
8" • Labrador Retriever • #2018
Issued: 1996 • Retired: 1996
Market Value: $55

(183) *New!*

Baby Patches™
12" • Dog • #2030
Issued: 1999 • Current
Market Value: $_____

(184)

Baby Schnapps™
N/A • Dog • #3001
Issued: 1986 • Retired: 1986
Market Value: N/E

DOGS

	Date Purchased	Price Paid	Value Of My Collection
181.			
182.			
183.			
184.			
PENCIL TOTALS			

DOGS

(185)

Baby Sparky™
20" • Dalmatian • #2012
Issued: 1992 • Retired: 1994
A. Tongue (1994)
B. No Tongue (1992-93)
Market Value: A/B–$145

(186)

Barney™
20" • Labrador Retriever • #2003
Issued: 1990 • Retired: 1992
Market Value: $775

(187)

Biscuit™
17" • Dog • #2026
Issued: 1997 • Retired: 1997
Market Value: $45

(188)

Bo™
20" • Basset Hound • #2009
Issued: 1994 • Retired: 1995
Market Value: $300

DOGS

	Date Purchased	Price Paid	Value Of My Collection
185.			
186.			
187.			
188.			
189.			
PENCIL TOTALS			

(189)

Buckshot™
20" • Basset Hound • #2009
Issued: 1992 • Retired: 1993
Market Value: $540

(190)

Buster™
20" • Cocker Spaniel • #2005
Issued: 1990 • Retired: 1991
Market Value: $650

(191)

Charlie™
20" • Cocker Spaniel • #2001
Issued: 1988 • Retired: 1990
A. Tongue (1990)
B. No Tongue (1988-89)
Market Value: A/B–$700

(192)

Charlie™
20" • Cocker Spaniel • #2005
Issued: 1994 • Retired: 1997
A. Floppy (1996-97)
B. Sitting (1994-95)
Market Value: A–$45 B–$70

(193)

Chips™
12" • Dog • #2025
Issued: 1997 • Current
Market Value: $_____

(194)

Churchill™
12" • Bulldog • #2017
Issued: 1996 • Current
Market Value: $_____

DOGS

	Date Purchased	Price Paid	Value Of My Collection
190.			
191.			
192.			
193.			
194.			
PENCIL TOTALS			

DOGS

(195)

Cinders™
20" • Labrador Retriever • #2008
Issued: 1994 • Retired: 1997
A. Sitting/Black & Brown (1995-97)
B. Floppy/All Black (1994)
Market Value: A/B–$65

(196)

Corky™
12" • Cocker Spaniel • #2023
Issued: 1996 • Current
Market Value: $_____

(197)

Dakota™
12" • Husky • #7418
Issued: 1995 • Current
A. 12"/Floppy (1998-Current)
B. 8"/Sitting (1997)
C. 12"/Sitting (1995-97)
Market Value: A–$_____   B–N/E C–$40

(198)

Dopey™
17" • Dog • #2022
Issued: 1996 • Retired: 1997
Market Value: $100

DOGS

	Date Purchased	Price Paid	Value Of My Collection
195.			
196.			
197.			
198.			
199.			
PENCIL TOTALS			

(199)

Droopy™
15" • Hound • #2009
Issued: 1996 • Retired: 1997
Market Value: $60

(200)

Elvis™
20" • Hound • #2010
Issued: 1995 • Retired: 1998
Market Value: $28

(201)

Fido™
8" • Dog • #2019
Issued: 1996 • Retired: 1996
Market Value: $55

(202)

Fritz™
20" • Dalmatian • #2002
Issued: 1988 • Retired: 1990
A. Tongue (1990)
B. No Tongue (1988-89)
Market Value: A/B–$380

(203)

Honey™
20" • Dog • #2001
Issued: 1995 • Retired: 1998
Market Value: $28

(204)

PHOTO
UNAVAILABLE

Large Max™
N/A • Dog • #9001
Issued: 1992 • Retired: 1992
Market Value: N/E

DOGS

	Date Purchased	Price Paid	Value Of My Collection
200.			
201.			
202.			
203.			
204.			
PENCIL TOTALS			

DOGS

(205)

Large Rusty™
26" • Mutt • #9011
Issued: 1994 • Retired: 1995
Market Value: $165

(206)

Large Scruffy™
26" • Dog • #9011
Issued: 1992 • Retired: 1993
Market Value: $230

(207)

Large Sparky™
26" • Dalmatian • #9002
Issued: 1992 • Retired: 1993
Market Value: $265

(208)

Max™
20" • Dog • #2008
Issued: 1991 • Retired: 1992
Market Value: $315

DOGS

	Date Purchased	Price Paid	Value Of My Collection
205.			
206.			
207.			
208.			
209.			
PENCIL TOTALS			

(209)

Max™
20" • Dog • #3001
Issued: 1988 • Retired: 1990
A. Tongue (1990)
B. No Tongue (1988-89)
Market Value: A/B–$910

(210)

Muffin™
13" • Dog • #2020
Issued: 1996 • Retired: 1998
Market Value: $19

(211)

Patches™
18" • Dog • #2003
Issued: 1996 • Current
Market Value: $_____

(212)

Pepper™
12" • Labrador Retriever • #2024
Issued: 1997 • Current
Market Value: $_____

(213)

Pierre™
10" • Poodle • #2004
Issued: 1995 • Retired: 1996
Market Value: $60

(214)

Rusty™
20" • Mutt • #2011
Issued: 1992 • Retired: 1996
Market Value: $55

DOGS

	Date Purchased	Price Paid	Value Of My Collection
210.			
211.			
212.			
213.			
214.			
PENCIL TOTALS			

DOGS

(215)

Sarge™
20" • German Shepherd • #2003
Issued: 1994 • Retired: 1995
Market Value: $375

(216)

Schnapps™
N/A • Dog • #3000
Issued: 1986 • Retired: 1986
Market Value: N/E

(217)

Scruffy™
20" • Dog • #2000
Issued: 1992 • Retired: 1996
A. Red Ribbon/White (1993-96)
B. Blue Ribbon/Cream (1992)
Market Value: A–$80 B–$185

(218)

Scruffy™
20" • Dog • #2001
Issued: 1991 • Retired: 1994
A. Ribbon (1992-94)
B. No Ribbon (1991)
Market Value: A/B–$155

DOGS

	Date Purchased	Price Paid	Value Of My Collection
215.			
216.			
217.			
218.			
219.			
PENCIL TOTALS			

(219)

Sherlock™
12" • Basset Hound • #2029
Issued: 1998 • Retired: 1998
Market Value: $17

(220)

Sniffles™
18" • Dog • #2021
Issued: 1996 • Retired: 1996
Market Value: $180

(221)

Spanky™
20" • St. Bernard • #2010
Issued: 1992 • Retired: 1993
Market Value: N/E

(222)

Spanky™
8" • Cocker Spaniel • #2015
Issued: 1996 • Retired: 1996
Market Value: $55

(223)

Sparky™
20" • Dalmatian • #2004
Issued: 1990 • Retired: 1993
Market Value: $230

DOGS

	Date Purchased	Price Paid	Value Of My Collection
220.			
221.			
222.			
223.			
PENCIL TOTALS			

Dogs

(224)

Sparky™
20" • Dalmatian • #2012
Issued: 1995 • Retired: 1995
Market Value: $160

(225)

Sunny™
14" • Dog • #2028
Issued: 1998 • Retired: 1998
Market Value: $15

(226)

Super Fritz™
36" • Dalmatian • #9002
Issued: 1989 • Retired: 1989
Market Value: $850

(227)

Super Max™
32" • Dog • #3002
Issued: 1988 • Retired: 1990
A. Tongue (1990)
B. No Tongue (1988-89)
Market Value: A/B-$700

Dogs

	Date Purchased	Price Paid	Value Of My Collection
224.			
225.			
226.			
227.			
228.			
PENCIL TOTALS			

(228)

Super Max™
26" • Dog • #9001
Issued: 1991 • Retired: 1992
A. 26" (1992)
B. 32" (1991)
Market Value: A/B-$600

(229)

Super Schnapps™
N/A • Dog • #3002
Issued: 1986 • Retired: 1986
Market Value: N/E

(230)

Super Scruffy™
32" • Dog • #9011
Issued: 1991 • Retired: 1991
Market Value: N/E

(231)

Super Sparky™
32" • Dalmatian • #9002
Issued: 1990 • Retired: 1991
Market Value: $550

(232)

Taffy™
12" • Terrier • #2014
Issued: 1996 • Current
A. 12" (1998-Current)
B. 8" (1996-97)
Market Value: A–$_____ B–$35

(233)

Timber™
20" • Husky • #2002
Issued: 1994 • Retired: 1998
Market Value: $28

DOGS

	Date Purchased	Price Paid	Value Of My Collection
229.			
230.			
231.			
232.			
233.			
PENCIL TOTALS			

Dogs

(234)

Toffee™
(announced as retired in 1998,
returned to production in 1999)
20" • Terrier • #2013
Issued: 1993 • Current
Market Value: $_____

(235)

Winston™
20" • Bulldog • #2007
Issued: 1991 • Current
Market Value: $_____

(236)

Yappy™
12" • Yorkshire Terrier • #2016
Issued: 1996 • Current
A. 12" (1998-Current)
B. 8" (1996-97)
Market Value: A–$_____ B–$40

(237)

Yorkie™
20" • Yorkshire Terrier • #2006
Issued: 1991 • Retired: 1996
Market Value: $75

Dogs

	Date Purchased	Price Paid	Value Of My Collection
234.			
235.			
236.			
237.			
PENCIL TOTALS			

COUNTRY

This collection of 55 animals from "down on the farm" includes cows, pigs and rabbits, amongst others. Currently, only nine of the animals are still available, including two which have donned sweaters and moved to *The Attic Treasures Collection*.

(238)

Angora™
14" • Rabbit • #8004
Issued: 1995 • Retired: 1995
Market Value: $105

(239)

Angora™
20" • Rabbit • #8005
Issued: 1991 • Retired: 1992
Market Value: $400

(240)

PHOTO UNAVAILABLE

Arnold™
20" • Pig • #6001
Issued: 1988 • Retired: 1989
Market Value: N/E

(241)

Arnold™
20" • Pig • #6002
Issued: 1990 • Retired: 1990
Market Value: $375

COUNTRY

	Date Purchased	Price Paid	Value Of My Collection
238.			
239.			
240.			
241.			
PENCIL TOTALS			

COUNTRY

(242)

Baby Clover™
12" • Cow • #8023
Issued: 1993 • Retired: 1994
Market Value: $110

(243)

Baby Curly Bunny™
12" • Bunny • #8024
Issued: 1993 • Retired: 1997
Market Value: $45

(244)

Baby Curly Bunny™
12" • Bunny • #8025
Issued: 1993 • Retired: 1997
Market Value: $40

(245)

Baby Lovie™
20" • Lamb • #8019
Issued: 1992 • Retired: 1992
Market Value: N/E

COUNTRY

	Date Purchased	Price Paid	Value Of My Collection
242.			
243.			
244.			
245.			
246.			
PENCIL TOTALS			

(246)

Baby Lovie™
12" • Lamb • #8020
Issued: 1993 • Retired: 1994
Market Value: $100

(247)

Baby Petunia™
12" • Pig • #8021
Issued: 1993 • Retired: 1994
A. Red Ribbon (1994)
B. Blue Ribbon (1993)
Market Value: A/B–$120

(248)

Baby Pokey™
13" • Rabbit • #8022
Issued: 1996 • Retired: 1997
Market Value: $35

(249)

Baby Smokey™
13" • Rabbit • #8023
Issued: 1996 • Retired: 1997
Market Value: $35

(250)

Bandit™
20" • Raccoon • #1119
Issued: 1990 • Retired: 1990
Market Value: $600

(251)

Beanie Bunny™
12" • Bunny • #8000
Issued: 1989 • Retired: 1992
Market Value: $725

COUNTRY

	Date Purchased	Price Paid	Value Of My Collection
247.			
248.			
249.			
250.			
251.			
PENCIL TOTALS			

COUNTRY

(252)

Beanie Bunny™
12" • Bunny • #8001
Issued: 1991 • Retired: 1992
Market Value: $725

(253)

Big Beanie Bunny™
15" • Bunny • #8011
Issued: 1990 • Retired: 1992
A. Gold Ribbon (1991-92)
B. Pink Ribbon (1990)
Market Value: A/B–$725

(254)

Big Beanie Bunny™
15" • Bunny • #8012
Issued: 1991 • Retired: 1992
Market Value: $725

(255)

Blossom™
18" • Rabbit • #8013
Issued: 1996 • Retired: 1997
Market Value: $90

COUNTRY

	Date Purchased	Price Paid	Value Of My Collection
252.			
253.			
254.			
255.			
256.			
PENCIL TOTALS			

(256)

Bows™
11" • Bunny • #8030
Issued: 1998 • Current
Market Value: $____

(257)

Buttercup™
18" • Rabbit • #8012
Issued: 1996 • Retired: 1997
Market Value: $115

(258)

Buttons™
11" • Bunny • #8031
Issued: 1998 • Current
Market Value: $_____

(259)

Candy™
N/A • Rabbit • #8011
Issued: 1996 • Retired: 1996
Market Value: $75

(260)

Chestnut™
12" • Squirrel • #8022
Issued: 1993 • Retired: 1993
Market Value: $160

(261)

Clover™
20" • Cow • #8007
Issued: 1991 • Retired: 1996
A. Ribbon (1996)
B. No Ribbon (1994-95)
C. Ribbon (1991-93)
Market Value: A/B/C–$85

COUNTRY

	Date Purchased	Price Paid	Value Of My Collection
257.			
258.			
259.			
260.			
261.			
PENCIL TOTALS			

COUNTRY

(262)

Cotton™
14" • Rabbit • #8003
Issued: 1996 • Retired: 1997
Market Value: $50

(263)

Curly Bunny™
(moved to Attic Treasures™ in 1999)
22" • Bunny • #8017
Issued: 1992 • Current
A. Sweater (1998-Current)
B. Ribbon (1992-98)
Market Value: A–$_____ B–N/E

(264)

Curly Bunny™
(moved to Attic Treasures™ in 1999)
22" • Bunny • #8018
Issued: 1992 • Current
A. Sweater (1998-Current)
B. Ribbon (1992-98)
Market Value: A–$_____ B–N/E

(265)

Domino™
20" • Rabbit • #8006
Issued: 1991 • Retired: 1992
Market Value: $450

COUNTRY

	Date Purchased	Price Paid	Value Of My Collection
262.			
263.			
264.			
265.			
266.			
PENCIL TOTALS			

(266)

Freddie™
12" • Frog • #1117
Issued: 1989 • Retired: 1990
A. 12" (1990)
B. 10" (1989)
Market Value: A/B–N/E

(267)

PHOTO UNAVAILABLE

Freddie™
N/A • Frog • #8002
Issued: 1989 • Retired: 1989
Market Value: N/E

(268)

Hooters™
9" • Owl • #8016
Issued: 1992 • Retired: 1994
Market Value: $400

(269)

Jersey™
20" • Cow • #8026
Issued: 1997 • Retired: 1998
A. Black & White (1997-98)
B. Brown & White (1997)
Market Value: A–$24 B–$45

(270)

Large Curly Bunny™
24" • Bunny • #9003
Issued: 1994 • Retired: 1997
Market Value: $80

COUNTRY

	Date Purchased	Price Paid	Value Of My Collection
267.			
268.			
269.			
270.			
PENCIL TOTALS			

COUNTRY

(271)

Large Curly Bunny™
24" • Bunny • #9007
Issued: 1996 • Retired: 1997
Market Value: $80

(272)

Large Petunia™
26" • Pig • #9003
Issued: 1992 • Retired: 1992
Market Value: $450

(273)

Lillie™
20" • Lamb • #8004
Issued: 1990 • Retired: 1990
Market Value: $550

(274)

Lovie™
18" • Lamb • #8001
Issued: 1988 • Retired: 1990
Market Value: $700

COUNTRY

	Date Purchased	Price Paid	Value Of My Collection
271.			
272.			
273.			
274.			
275.			
PENCIL TOTALS			

(275)

Lovie™
20" • Lamb • #8004
Issued: 1991 • Retired: 1993
Market Value: $430

276

Lovie™
20" • Lamb • #8019
Issued: 1993 • Retired: 1996
Market Value: $125

277

Lovie™
**(announced as retired in 1998,
returned to production in 1999)**
10" • Lamb • #8027
Issued: 1998 • Current
Market Value: $_____

278

Nibbles™
9" • Bunny • #8000
Issued: 1994 • Current
Market Value: $_____

279

Nibbles™
9" • Bunny • #8001
Issued: 1995 • Current
Market Value: $_____

COUNTRY

	Date Purchased	Price Paid	Value Of My Collection
276.			
277.			
278.			
279.			
PENCIL TOTALS			

COUNTRY

(280)

Peepers™
9" • Chick • #8015
Issued: 1991 • Retired: 1994
A. Feet (1992-94)
B. No Feet (1991)
Market Value: A/B–$160

(281)

Peter™
14" • Rabbit • #8002
Issued: 1989 • Retired: 1997
A. 14"/Jointed (1996-97)
B. 20"/Not Jointed (1989-94)
Market Value: A–$60 B–$330

(282)

Petunia™
20" • Pig • #6001
Issued: 1989 • Retired: 1990
Market Value: $480

(283)

Petunia™
20" • Pig • #8008
Issued: 1991 • Retired: 1995
A. Red Ribbon (1994-95)
B. Blue Ribbon (1993)
C. Pink Ribbon (1991-92)
Market Value: A–$130 B–$145 C–$170

COUNTRY

	Date Purchased	Price Paid	Value Of My Collection
280.			
281.			
282.			
283.			
284.			
PENCIL TOTALS			

(284)

Pokey™
19" • Rabbit • #8015
Issued: 1996 • Retired: 1997
Market Value: $65

(285)

Rosie™
20" • Rabbit • #8003
Issued: 1990 • Retired: 1994
Market Value: $420

(286)

Smokey™
19" • Rabbit • #8016
Issued: 1996 • Retired: 1997
Market Value: $55

(287)

Sparkles™
20" • Unicorn • #8100
Issued: 1997 • Current
A. Multi-Color Mane & Tail (1999-Current)
B. Pink Mane & Tail (1997-98)
Market Value: A–$_____ B–N/E

(288)

Super Arnold™
32" • Pig • #9003
Issued: 1990 • Retired: 1990
Market Value: N/E

(289)

Super Petunia™
32" • Pig • #9003
Issued: 1989 • Retired: 1991
A. 32"/Ribbon (1991)
B. 36"/No Ribbon (1989)
Market Value: A/B–N/E

COUNTRY

	Date Purchased	Price Paid	Value Of My Collection
285.			
286.			
287.			
288.			
289.			
PENCIL TOTALS			

COUNTRY

(290)

Tulip™
18" • Pig • #8008
Issued: 1996 • Retired: 1998
Market Value: $26

(291)

Whinnie™
20" • Horse • #8006
Issued: 1994 • Retired: 1995
Market Value: $270

(292)

Woolly™
9" • Lamb • #8005
Issued: 1996 • Current
Market Value: $_____

Country

	Date Purchased	Price Paid	Value Of My Collection
290.			
291.			
292.			
PENCIL TOTALS			

WILDLIFE

Take a walk on the wild side with *Ty Plush* wildlife! This collection of jungle creatures includes everything from chimps to cheetahs. Of the 66 pieces in the collection, 58 have crept into retirement.

(293)

Arctic™
12" • Polar Bear • #7419
Issued: 1995 • Retired: 1997
Market Value: $55

(294)

Baby George™
12" • Gorilla • #7300
Issued: 1996 • Retired: 1998
Market Value: $14

(295)

Bandit™
20" • Raccoon • #8009
Issued: 1991 • Retired: 1996
A. Brown (1992-96)
B. Gray (1991)
Market Value: A–$80 B–$475

(296)

Bengal™
12" • Tiger • #7423
Issued: 1995 • Current
A. Floppy/Gold Chest (1998-Current)
B. Sitting/White Chest (1995-97)
Market Value: A–$_____ B–$42

WILDLIFE

	Date Purchased	Price Paid	Value Of My Collection
293.			
294.			
295.			
296.			
PENCIL TOTALS			

WILDLIFE

Big George™
27" • Gorilla • #7302
Issued: 1990 • Current
Market Value: $_____

Big Jake™
16" • Monkey • #7002
Issued: 1989 • Retired: 1989
Market Value: $400

Big Jake™
16" • Monkey • #7002A
Issued: 1989 • Retired: 1989
Market Value: $425

Big Jake™
16" • Monkey • #7002C
Issued: 1989 • Retired: 1989
Market Value: $425

WILDLIFE

	Date Purchased	Price Paid	Value Of My Collection
297.			
298.			
299.			
300.			
301.			
PENCIL TOTALS			

Big Jake™
16" • Monkey • #7200
Issued: 1990 • Retired: 1990
Market Value: N/E

(302)

Big Jake™
16" • Monkey • #7201
Issued: 1990 • Retired: 1990
Market Value: $400

(303)

Big Jake™
16" • Monkey • #7202
Issued: 1990 • Retired: 1990
Market Value: N/E

(304)

Cha Cha™
12" • Monkey • #7005
Issued: 1998 • Current
Market Value: $_____

(305)

Chi-Chi™
20" • Cheetah • #1114
Issued: 1989 • Retired: 1990
A. No Ribbon (1990)
B. Ribbon (1989)
Market Value: A/B–$860

(306)

Chi-Chi™
20" • Cheetah • #7414
Issued: 1991 • Retired: 1992
Market Value: $620

WILDLIFE

	Date Purchased	Price Paid	Value Of My Collection
302.			
303.			
304.			
305.			
306.			
PENCIL TOTALS			

WILDLIFE

307

Chuckles™
15" • Chimp • #7303
Issued: 1997 • Retired: 1997
Market Value: $55

308

Elmer™
20" • Elephant • #1116
Issued: 1989 • Retired: 1990
A. No Ribbon (1990)
B. Ribbon (1989)
Market Value: A/B–$770

309

Elmer™
20" • Elephant • #7416
Issued: 1991 • Retired: 1996
A. Gray Ears/Long Trunk (1994-96)
B. White Ears/Short Trunk (1991-93)
Market Value: A–$125   B–$320

310

Freddie™
16" • Frog • #8010
Issued: 1991 • Retired: 1998
A. 16" (1995-98)
B. 12" (1991)
Market Value: A–$28   B–N/E

WILDLIFE

	Date Purchased	Price Paid	Value Of My Collection
307.			
308.			
309.			
310.			
311.			
PENCIL TOTALS			

311

George™
20" • Gorilla • #7301
Issued: 1990 • Current
Market Value: $_____

(312)

Harris™
20" • Lion • #1115
Issued: 1989 • Retired: 1990
A. Gold & Tan Mane (1990)
B. Gold Mane (1989)
Market Value: A/B–N/E

(313)

Harris™
20" • Lion • #7415
Issued: 1991 • Retired: 1996
Market Value: $85

(314)

Jake™
12" • Monkey • #7001
Issued: 1988 • Retired: 1989
Market Value: $700

(315)

Jake™
12" • Monkey • #7001A
Issued: 1989 • Retired: 1989
Market Value: $700

(316)

Jake™
N/A • Monkey • #7001B
Issued: 1989 • Retired: 1989
Market Value: N/E

WILDLIFE

	Date Purchased	Price Paid	Value Of My Collection
312.			
313.			
314.			
315.			
316.			
PENCIL TOTALS			

WILDLIFE

(317)

Jake™
12" • Monkey • #7001C
Issued: 1989 • Retired: 1989
Market Value: $700

(318)

Jake™
N/A • Monkey • #7001R
Issued: 1989 • Retired: 1989
Market Value: N/E

(319)

Jake™
24" • Monkey • #7100
Issued: 1990 • Retired: 1994
A. 24" (1992-94)
B. 22" (1991)
C. 12" (1990)
Market Value: A–$320 B–$320 C–N/E

(320)

Jake™
24" • Monkey • #7101
Issued: 1990 • Retired: 1993
A. 24" (1992-93)
B. 22" (1991)
C. 12" (1990)
Market Value: A–$300 B–$300 C–N/E

WILDLIFE

	Date Purchased	Price Paid	Value Of My Collection
317.			
318.			
319.			
320.			
321.			
PENCIL TOTALS			

(321)

Jake™
12" • Monkey • #7102
Issued: 1990 • Retired: 1990
Market Value: N/E

(322)

Josh™
24" • Monkey • #7101
Issued: 1994 • Retired: 1996
Market Value: $125

(323)

Jumbo George™
48" • Gorilla • #9008
Issued: 1991 • Current
Market Value: $_____

(324)

Leo™
22" • Lion • #7427
Issued: 1997 • Retired: 1998
Market Value: $24

(325)

Mango™
20" • Monkey • #7100
Issued: 1995 • Retired: 1998
Market Value: $24

(326)

Mango™
20" • Monkey • #7102
Issued: 1995 • Retired: 1998
Market Value: $24

WILDLIFE

	Date Purchased	Price Paid	Value Of My Collection
322.			
323.			
324.			
325.			
326.			
PENCIL TOTALS			

WILDLIFE

(327)

Mischief™
18" • Monkey • #7000
Issued: 1988 • Retired: 1993
A. White (1991-93)
B. Auburn (1990)
C. White (1988-89)
Market Value: A–$330 B–N/E C–$330

(328)

Mischief™
18" • Monkey • #7000A
Issued: 1989 • Retired: 1989
Market Value: $450

(329)

Mischief™
N/A • Monkey • #7000B
Issued: 1989 • Retired: 1989
Market Value: $450

(330)

Mischief™
18" • Monkey • #7000C
Issued: 1989 • Retired: 1989
Market Value: $450

WILDLIFE

	Date Purchased	Price Paid	Value Of My Collection
327.			
328.			
329.			
330.			
331.			
PENCIL TOTALS			

(331)

Mischief™
N/A • Monkey • #7000R
Issued: 1989 • Retired: 1989
Market Value: N/E

(332)

Mischief ™
18" • Monkey • #7001
Issued: 1990 • Retired: 1993
A. Auburn (1991-93)
B. White (1990)
Market Value: A–$320 B–N/E

(333)

Mischief ™
18" • Monkey • #7002
Issued: 1990 • Retired: 1991
Market Value: N/E

(334)

Mischief™
21" • Monkey • #7414
Issued: 1996 • Retired: 1997
Market Value: $120

(335)

Misty™
14" • Seal • #7400
Issued: 1991 • Retired: 1994
A. 14"/Ribbon (1993-94)
B. 12"/No Ribbon (1991-92)
Market Value: A/B–$185

WILDLIFE

	Date Purchased	Price Paid	Value Of My Collection
332.			
333.			
334.			
335.			
PENCIL TOTALS			

WILDLIFE

(336)

Misty™
11" • Seal • #7431
Issued: 1998 • Current
Market Value: $_____

(337)

Mortimer™
18" • Moose • #7417
Issued: 1996 • Retired: 1998
Market Value: $23

(338)

Otto™
20" • Otter • #7417
Issued: 1993 • Retired: 1994
Market Value: $240

(339)

Patti™
20" • Panther • #1118
Issued: 1989 • Retired: 1990
A. No Ribbon (1990)
B. Ribbon (1989)
Market Value: A/B–$800

WILDLIFE

	Date Purchased	Price Paid	Value Of My Collection
336.			
337.			
338.			
339.			
340.			
PENCIL TOTALS			

(340)

Rascal™
16" • Monkey • #7001
Issued: 1994 • Retired: 1997
Market Value: $50

(341)

Sahara™
12" • Lion • #7421
Issued: 1995 • Current
A. Floppy/Gold Chest/Long Mane
(1998-Current)
B. Sitting/Gold Chest/Long Mane (1996)
C. Sitting/White Chest/Short Mane (1995)
Market Value: A–$_____ B–$40 C–$40

(342)

Shivers™
9" • Penguin • #7419
Issued: 1993 • Retired: 1994
Market Value: $350

(343)

Spout™
9" • Elephant • #7426
Issued: 1996 • Current
A. Floppy (1998-Current)
B. Sitting (1996-97)
Market Value: A–$_____ B–$35

(344)

Super Chi-Chi™
52" • Cheetah • #9004
Issued: 1989 • Retired: 1989
Market Value: $825

(345)

Super George™
38" • Gorilla • #9007
Issued: 1990 • Retired: 1991
Market Value: $640

WILDLIFE

	Date Purchased	Price Paid	Value Of My Collection
341.			
342.			
343.			
344.			
345.			
PENCIL TOTALS			

(346)

Super Jake™
16" • Monkey • #7002
Issued: 1988 • Retired: 1989
Market Value: $900

(347)

Super Jake™
N/A • Monkey • #7002B
Issued: 1989 • Retired: 1989
Market Value: N/E

(348)

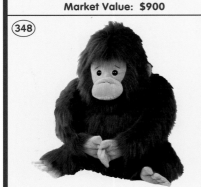

Super Jake™
N/A • Monkey • #7002R
Issued: 1989 • Retired: 1989
Market Value: N/E

(349)

Super Jake™
55" • Monkey • #9001
Issued: 1989 • Retired: 1989
Market Value: $900

WILDLIFE

	Date Purchased	Price Paid	Value Of My Collection
346.			
347.			
348.			
349.			
350.			
PENCIL TOTALS			

(350)

Super Tygger™
32" • Tiger • #9004
Issued: 1990 • Retired: 1991
Market Value: N/E

(351)

Tango™
12" • Monkey • #7000
Issued: 1995 • Retired: 1998
Market Value: $24

(352)

Tango™
12" • Monkey • #7002
Issued: 1995 • Retired: 1998
Market Value: $24

(353)

Twiggy™
23" • Giraffe • #7422
Issued: 1991 • Retired: 1996
Market Value: $125

(354)

Tygger™
20" • Tiger • #1120
Issued: 1990 • Retired: 1990
Market Value: N/E

(355)

Tygger™
20" • Tiger • #7420
Issued: 1991 • Retired: 1998
A. Floppy (1994-98)
B. Standing (1992-93)
C. Floppy (1991)
Market Value: A–$28 B–$250 C–N/E

WILDLIFE

	Date Purchased	Price Paid	Value Of My Collection
351.			
352.			
353.			
354.			
355.			
PENCIL TOTALS			

WILDLIFE

(356)

Tygger™
20" • Tiger • #7421
Issued: 1991 • Retired: 1992
Market Value: $400

(357)

Wally™
12" • Walrus • #7423
Issued: 1992 • Retired: 1993
Market Value: $165

(358)

Zulu™
20" • Zebra • #7421
Issued: 1994 • Retired: 1994
Market Value: $405

WILDLIFE

	Date Purchased	Price Paid	Value Of My Collection
356.			
357.			
358.			
PENCIL TOTALS			

Use these pages to record future Ty® Plush releases.

Ty® PLUSH	Date Purchased	Price Paid	Value Of My Collection
PENCIL TOTALS			

Ty® PLUSH

TOTAL VALUE OF MY COLLECTION

Record the value of your collection here by adding the
pencil totals from the bottom of each Value Guide page.

ATTIC TREASURES™			BEANIE BABIES®		
Page Number	Price Paid	Market Value	Page Number	Price Paid	Market Value
Page 39			Page 68		
Page 40			Page 69		
Page 41			Page 70		
Page 42			Page 71		
Page 43			Page 72		
Page 44			Page 73		
Page 45			Page 74		
Page 46			Page 75		
Page 47			Page 76		
Page 48			Page 77		
Page 49			Page 78		
Page 50			Page 79		
Page 51			Page 80		
Page 52			Page 81		
Page 53			Page 82		
Page 54			Page 83		
Page 55			Page 84		
Page 56			Page 85		
Page 57			Page 86		
Page 58			Page 87		
Page 59			Page 88		
Page 60			Page 89		
Page 61			Page 90		
Page 62			Page 91		
Page 63			Page 92		
Page 64			Page 93		
BEANIE BABIES®			Page 94		
			Page 95		
Page 65			Page 96		
Page 66			Page 97		
Page 67			Page 98		
TOTAL			TOTAL		

TOTAL VALUE OF MY COLLECTION

Record the value of your collection here by adding the
pencil totals from the bottom of each Value Guide page.

BEANIE BABIES®		
Page Number	Price Paid	Market Value
Page 99		
Page 100		
Page 101		
Page 102		
Page 103		
Page 104		
Page 105		
Page 106		
Page 107		
Page 108		
Page 109		

BEANIE BUDDIES®		
Page 110		
Page 111		
Page 112		
Page 113		
Page 114		
Page 115		
Page 116		

TEENIE BEANIE BABIES™		
Page 117		
Page 118		
Page 119		
Page 120		
Page 121		

PILLOW PALS™		
Page 122		
Page 123		
Page 124		
Page 125		
Page 126		
TOTAL		

PILLOW PALS™		
Page Number	Price Paid	Market Value
Page 126		
Page 127		
Page 128		
Page 129		
Page 130		
Page 131		
Page 132		

TY® PLUSH		
Page 133		
Page 134		
Page 135		
Page 136		
Page 137		
Page 138		
Page 139		
Page 140		
Page 141		
Page 142		
Page 143		
Page 144		
Page 145		
Page 146		
Page 147		
Page 148		
Page 149		
Page 150		
Page 151		
Page 152		
Page 153		
Page 154		
Page 155		
TOTAL		

TOTAL VALUE OF MY COLLECTION

Record the value of your collection here by adding the
pencil totals from the bottom of each Value Guide page.

TY® PLUSH			TY® PLUSH		
Page Number	Price Paid	Market Value	Page Number	Price Paid	Market Value
Page 156			Page 183		
Page 157			Page 184		
Page 158			Page 185		
Page 159			Page 186		
Page 160			Page 187		
Page 161			Page 188		
Page 162			Page 189		
Page 163			Page 190		
Page 164			Page 191		
Page 165			Page 192		
Page 166			Page 193		
Page 167			Page 194		
Page 168			Page 195		
Page 169			Page 196		
Page 170			Page 197		
Page 171			Page 198		
Page 172			Page 199		
Page 173			Page 200		
Page 174			Page 201		
Page 175			Page 202		
Page 176			Page 203		
Page 177			Page 204		
Page 178			Page 205		
Page 179			Page 206		
Page 180			Page 207		
Page 181			Page 208		
Page 182			Page 209		
TOTAL			TOTAL		

GRAND TOTALS		
	PRICE PAID	MARKET VALUE

*W*hat do you need to know about the secondary market and what strategies are valuable in the hunt for the Ty pieces you are looking for? First of all, you should understand WHY there is a demand for certain pieces and then find out WHERE to go in your search for them.

NOT EXACTLY A TIME OF REST

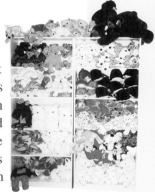

Collectors whose ultimate goal is to acquire a complete set of a particular Ty collection will discover that a number of pieces have disappeared from the shelves of the local gift shop or the kiosk at the local mall. Why? Usually, these pieces have been "retired," meaning that they have been taken out of production, never to be produced again. Such retirements occur so that room can be made in the collection for new introductions. As these newly designed pieces take their positions on the store shelves, the older, retired animals are eventually sold out and the hunt for these pieces begins. And as they become more and more difficult to find, their value starts to increase, at times quite significantly.

While most retirements are officially acknowledged by Ty Inc., many pieces, including rare older pieces and variations, slip quietly away without any fanfare. The most up-to-date and accurate source for this type of information is the official company Internet web site, www.ty.com.

NOT JUST ONE IN A CROWD

A number of the animals created by Ty have appeared in a variety of colors, designs, fabrics, names and sizes and are commonly known as "variations." Whether these differences are due to human error or a deliberate change in production, collectors who want a "complete" collection will search high and low for these rare and difficult-to-locate pieces.

Secondary Market Overview

Very, very lucky collectors may find these altered characters on a store shelf but for most, the only place to track them down is on the secondary market. Unfortunately, it is impossible to determine what affect a variation will have on the market value of a particular piece. For more information, see the *Variations* section on page 218.

A Little TLC Goes A Long Way!

The general condition of a Ty plush animal is important when being considered for swap or sale. If your primary goal in collecting is to eventually sell the piece for monetary profit, you must ensure that it remains in like-new condition. In other words, lollipops and soda pop should never be introduced to a plush's diet and a smoke-free environment is the healthiest bet for all!

Additionally, the presence and condition of the swing and tush tags are extremely vital in the Ty plush secondary market. Used primarily as an identification tool, intact tags are also used as an indication of whether the piece was cared for and kept safe from excessive handling and dirt. The tags for some of the Ty collections have gone through many transformations throughout the years. The chronology of different tag versions – commonly referred to as "generations" – can help determine the approximate age of the plush piece. For *Attic Treasures* and *Beanie Babies* pieces, the earliest released pieces with attached tags are the ones usually considered to be the most valuable. However, in order to maintain the full secondary market value, all pieces must retain both tags in like-new, mint condition. For more specific suggestions on how to protect your investment, check out the *Protecting And Insuring Your Collection* section on page 234.

TRACKING DOWN THE TY GUYS

In an effort to continue providing a variety of stuffed plush at affordable prices to animal lovers worldwide, Ty periodically releases newly designed versions of both old and new favorites. Like with almost anything, shortage creates demand and there never seems to be enough Ty plush animals to keep all the collectors satisfied. With *Beanie Babies,* and now with the new and highly sought-after *Beanie Buddies*, some avid collectors are more than willing to pay inflated prices on the secondary market just to ensure that they have every piece that has been issued even though these pieces will eventually appear on retail store shelves with a more moderate price tag. And the hunt doesn't stop there. Often, there can be frenzied dashes to the local gift shop when a rumor circulates of UPS delivery truck sightings and dedicated collectors may also develop an itinerary of favorite stores to frequent in their hunt for desired pieces. The best strategy, however, is to be patient in your search and be pleasantly surprised when you do spot a dark blue "Peanut" *Beanie Baby* on a dusty store shelf at your favorite vacation spot!

THE SECONDARY MARKET SCENE

Now that you know what can affect the value of Ty plush animals on the secondary market, your next question is "Where can I go to buy or sell my Ty pieces?" There are a variety of options that you can choose from, and you should carefully look at more than one in order to select the best method for you. While some collectors prefer to deal with a "live" person on the telephone or have a "face-to-face" meeting with a trusted and recommended dealer, many collectors have discovered that the Internet is a valuable resource to meet their shopping needs.

TY GOES "HIGH-TECH"

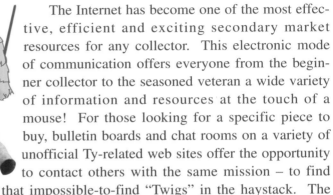

The Internet has become one of the most effective, efficient and exciting secondary market resources for any collector. This electronic mode of communication offers everyone from the beginner collector to the seasoned veteran a wide variety of information and resources at the touch of a mouse! For those looking for a specific piece to buy, bulletin boards and chat rooms on a variety of unofficial Ty-related web sites offer the opportunity to contact others with the same mission – to find that impossible-to-find "Twigs" in the haystack. The Internet offers convenience, instantaneous results, secure shopping and vast amounts of information.

There are many other avenues to turn down while exploring the Internet. Many retail stores now have their own web sites where Ty products are offered for sale. Orders are taken and transactions are conducted with the touch of a few keys and an e-mail address. Internet auction sites also provide a convenient method of browsing, visually inspecting and shopping for items that are available. You can conduct a search for Ty pieces in general or be specific in your quest. Although most transactions made over the Internet are problem-free, one should become familiar with the procedure used for the variety of shopping options. Be an informed collector.

ADS CAN ADD UP TO SUCCESS!

Another way to reach Ty collectors, especially in your immediate locale, is through your hometown newspaper's classified advertisement section. Many newspapers now feature a section specifically for *Beanie Babies* and other Ty products. To reach a more specific group of collectors, however, you might have better luck looking in the "swap & sell" sections of collectibles newsletters and magazines.

VISIT YOUR FRIENDLY LOCAL RETAILER

Although most retailers do not participate in the secondary market, some may be able to act as a liaison between you and other collectors who share the same interests. Often they can provide you with a list of other collectors looking to buy or sell certain pieces, as well as information concerning swap & sells in your area which can be excellent places to meet other collectors looking to buy, sell or trade pieces. Often, this is where you may find true experts in the field who may be able to answer your questions about collecting Ty plush animals.

WHAT WOULD YOUR GRANDCHILDREN SAY?

While the secondary market is a great way to add to your collection, there is no guarantee that you will benefit monetarily. In this nebulous, volatile market, the willingness to take chances must be a part of your investment strategy.

For many people, the reason for collecting Ty plush animals is a balance between the intriguing "collectibility" and potential value of the pieces and the genuine joy they feel when looking at (and playing with) their collection. It's easy to get caught up in the the collecting frenzy, but the following tips can be very helpful for collectors: stay informed, set goals, be patient, have fun and enjoy the challenge. Your quest for the perfect collection should be motivated with those things in mind. Then the tales you tell your grandchildren about your "Ty" days will be funny and exciting, including stories about your weekly trips to McDonald's when you "ate over 25 Happy Meals!"

VARIATIONS

E ver notice that day in, day out, it seems like the same old thing? Well, many of the members of the Ty plush animal family have noticed and aren't ready to give in to this humdrum existence. Instead, they have decided to make some changes.

When a collectible undergoes a change, it is known as a variation. Sometimes this involves a subtle alteration, while other times, the modification is quite obvious. These variations can be due to a number of reasons, including human error or a conscious decision to change the piece. Whatever the cause and whatever the degree, finding a variation is a great source of excitement for many collectors.

Often, variations become highly sought-after and soar in value on the secondary market. Other times, they become nothing more than a point of interest. So while it is nearly impossible to determine just what effect a variation will have on the worth of the piece, there are some specific changes that, more than likely, will enhance its value.

SUITED TO THE "T"

The characters of *Attic Treasures*, as well as a few of the plush animals, know that not only does clothing make the man, but it also makes the bear, the cat, the rabbit and even the hippo. So while many of these pieces were originally produced without clothing, or with only a ribbon around their neck, most of the more recent pieces have stepped into the fashion spotlight and are donning some pretty stylish outfits.

After one year of production, "Justin" the *Attic Treasures* monkey, decided to put on a sweater for a year before retiring. Others, such as "Jeremy" the rabbit weren't sure what style best suited them and tried on a variety of outfits before settling on one. And then there are those like "Dickens," who decided after trying on clothes for a while, that the natural look is much more comfortable. In the plush animal collection, "Baby Curly" and some of his close relatives decided not only that it was getting a bit too cold being "bare" and put on sweaters, but also to make a change in habitat, as they crawled into *The Attic Treasures Collection.*

Sometimes, the animal decides that his particular style is just fine, but is looking for some variation. The plush "Romeo" sported ribbons adorned with different sayings. However, ribbon changes such as this normally do not command a significantly higher value on the secondary market.

One should always exercise caution when seeking out this type of variation. While the animals wearing no clothing often command a higher value on the secondary market, it is more likely a result of these designs being among the first produced (see *Swing Tags* section on page 224 for more information), rather than the fact that they are undressed. Remember, it is not difficult to make a bear that is currently being produced with clothing, appear to be the earlier, undressed version with the removal of the tell-tale sweater.

NOT THE SAME OLD HUE

A color change is not usually one of the more subtle of the variations. However, it doesn't have to be as dramatic as the introduction of the new vibrant hues of the *Pillow Pals* to be of interest.

For example, the change of skin that the *Beanie Babies* "Iggy" and "Rainbow" underwent caused quite a stir among collectors. After a few months of production in a case of "the grass seems greener on the other side of the fence," these lizards decided that they were much better suited in each other's coat and traded. So current versions of "Iggy" sport a blue hue, while the current ver-

VARIATIONS

sions of "Rainbow" wear a fittingly tie-dyed suit.

The *Ty Plush* cow "Jersey" didn't seem to heed much attention to her name. While she was originally brown and white (a trait characteristic of her type), she decided that she wanted to stand out amidst the herd of Jersey cows and changed her fur to black and white.

TWO FACED (OR BODIED)

Probably the most obvious of the variations is one that could actually go unnoticed because the change is so dramatic that many people may not recognize the different versions as actually being the same piece. This type of variation is the design change.

Often when a design change occurs, the animal's style number and name remain the same, but the physical attributes of the animal undergo a complete transformation.

The most well-known example of this type of change is the case of the "old face" and "new face" versions of "Teddy" the *Beanie Baby*. Originally produced with pointed snouts and widely spaced eyes, these bears experienced a rounding out of the face, so to speak. While the original versions are highly valuable, the revised versions have also made a big hit on the collectible scene as many recent bear introductions are modeled in this fashion.

In another extreme example, in 1996, the *Ty Plush* rabbit "Peter" acquired a more realistic look with alterations to his body (which became jointed), face and ears.

However, not all of these types of changes are quite as noticeable. Many of the *Ty Plush* animals also underwent alterations in their body style that affected the

position in which they sit (understandable for anyone who knows what it's like to stay in one position for too long). "Al E. Kat" curled up after a few years of just lying around flat, while others such as "Dakota" relaxed a bit and flopped around after a few years of sitting. "Elmer," the elephant's trunk grew and "Fritz" realized that, since he is a dog, it is okay for him to walk around with his tongue hanging out.

A BRAND NEW SKIN

A less noticeable change occurs when an animal tires of the fabric of its coat and opts for a new one. At times, this involves the material of the entire piece while at others, it could be just a small feature, such as a change in the whiskers or the mane.

Recently, the *Beanie Babies* "Derby" and "Mystic," both of whom have been through a variety of mane styles, softened their formerly coarse manes, opting for more fluffy coifs.

Usually, this type of variation does not command a significantly higher value on the secondary market. This is sometimes due to simple production factors, such as when a new batch of fabric with a slight color variance is used in the production of a piece.

HI, MY NAME IS...

A few of the animals in the Ty family have pondered the question, "What's in a name?" and, as a result, have decided to change theirs. For example, the *Beanie Baby* "Doodle" became "Strut" after a few months of production.

A more valuable variation of this type also occurs within the *Beanie Babies* family. In 1995,

Bongo ™ style 4067

to _____

from _____

with

love

Nana ™ style 4067

to _____

from _____

with

love

VARIATIONS

"Nana" changed his name to "Bongo" and even though originally the piece was physically the same (although a few months later its tail underwent a color change), it has proven to be quite valuable on the secondary market.

WITH THE PROPER AMOUNT OF WATER AND SUNLIGHT . . .

Much like the collectors who love them, many of the *Ty Plush* characters have grown (and even shrunk) over their life span. "Yappy" grew about four inches since her birth, while on the other hand, "Super Petunia" became four inches smaller.

A STITCH IN TIME

Depending on the point in an animal's life span, it may sport different styles of stitching. This may include changes in the actual color of the stitching itself, such as the the various shades of pink thread used on the *Beanie Baby* "Magic."

As one of the more subtle changes, an alteration in stitching often goes unnoticed. However, luckily for the keen eye, it often does command a higher value on the secondary market.

A SOMETIMES VALUABLE INCONSISTENCY

It is not uncommon to find an error on an animal's swing tag. These errors can occur in several manners, ranging from a misspelling in a *Beanie Babies* poem to a misspelling of some of the other information printed on the tag. Recently, some critters have been sporting tags that give the incorrect

SAFETY PRECAUTION
Please remove all tags and other accessories before giving to a child under 3 years of age.

0 08421 06082 5
Return Tag For Reference
Surface
Wash

SAFETY PRECAUTION
Please remove all tags and other accessories before giving to a child under 3 years of age.

0 08421 06069 6
Retain Tag For Reference
Surface
Wash

instruction "Return tag for reference," when the proper instruction is to "Retain" the tag.

In many cases, the swing (and sometimes tush) tag on the animal actually belongs to a different member of the family. The switching of the *Beanie Babies* "Echo" and "Waves" tags is a well-known and widespread example.

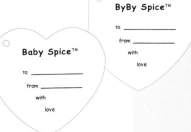

A less dramatic error, but one which also involves a situation of mistaken identity, occurs in the misspelling of the animal's name. "Spooky" the *Beanie Baby* is occasionally known to sport a highly valuable "Spook" tag, while some of the *Ty Plush* "Baby Spice" bears wear a "ByBy Spice" swing tag. As is often the case with this type of variation, the latter does not have a significant value difference over the correct version.

A WORLD OF DIFFERENCE

There are so many variations in the world of Ty plush animals that it is impossible to keep track of them all, let alone predict which ones will command a higher value on the secondary market. However, just knowing that these are out there adds a whole other dimension to the fun of collecting. When discovering those that do exist, collectors should never lose sight of the fact that while a high value is definitely a good thing, collecting should always be fun!

SWING TAGS

*T*y Warner and his menagerie of stuffed animals have undoubtedly revolutionized the collectibles market during the past decade. The tags that he attached to his stuffed toys in the late 1980s were merely for identification purposes at the retail level and provided a location where a price tag could be placed. If only we knew how important these tags would be in the future! These innocuous paper tags are now used not only for identification purposes, but also for determining secondary market value through a progression of tag "generations."

The condition and presence of the Ty swing tag is just as important as the condition of the piece itself. The tag can help determine whether the animal is an authentic Ty product and can also assist in estimating the age of the piece since the tags have undergone a specific and documented series of design changes. The earliest tag versions are considered by many collectors to be the most valuable since the animals that are attached to them are the pieces that were the earliest productions of the Ty collections.

ATTIC TREASURES SWING TAGS

Generation 1: The premiere *Attic Treasures* featured tags with no fold and have the word "ty" printed on the front in a skinny font. Both the word and the tag itself are outlined in gold. Additionally, tags attached to the "Woolie" bears also have the words "100% WOOL" printed on a diagonal in the upper right-hand corner.

The Attic Treasures Collection
Emily ™ - Style 6016
© 1992 Ty Inc. Oakbrook, IL USA
Designed by: Nola Hart
All Rights Reserved. Caution
Remove this tag before giving
toy to a child. For ages 5 and up.
Printed in Korea
Handmade in China
Surface
Wash

On the back of the tag, information listing the name of the collection, the name of the piece, the style number, cautionary remarks regarding the tag, cleaning instructions and where the piece was made. If the animal was one of those designed by either Linda Harris or Ruth Fraser, the artist's signature facsimile may also be found on the back.

Generation 2: The front of the tag is identical to the Generation 1 version, however, it now opens like a book. On the inside of the tag, the collection name is printed on the left side with company information and care instructions. On the right

> The Attic Treasures Collection
> © 1993 Ty Inc. Oakbrook IL. USA
> All Rights Reserved, Caution:
> Remove this tag before giving
> toy to a child. For ages 3 and up.
> Handmade in China
> Surface
> Wash.
>
> Cassie ™ style 6028
> to _____
> from _____
> with love

side, the animal's name and style number appears above a section to be used for gift-giving which says "to/from/with love." On the back, the UPC (Universal Product Code) information is found with a reminder to retain the tag for reference.

Generation 3: These tags were used briefly and featured a change only in the font size used for the Ty letters on the tag's front. The two letters were "puffed up" to the familiar logo used today.

> The Attic Treasures Collection
> © 1993 Ty Inc. Oakbrook IL. USA
> All Rights Reserved, Caution:
> Remove this tag before giving
> toy to a child. For ages 3 and up.
> Handmade in China
> Surface
> Wash.
>
> Emily ™ style 6018
> to _____
> from _____
> with love

Generation 4: The outside of the fourth generation tag is identical in design to its predecessor except for a green stripe with the word "collectible" which was added diagonally across the upper right hand corner. Ty production locations were added

> Ty Collectibles ™
> © Ty Inc.
> Oakbrook IL. U.S.A.
> Ty UK Ltd.
> Waterlooville, Hants
> P08 8HH
> Ty Deutschland
> 90008 Nürnberg
> Handmade in China
>
> Jeremy ™ style 6008
> to _____
> from _____
> with love

to the inside left while the information on care and caution were moved to the back. Additionally, the collection's name now is noted as "Ty Collectibles™."

Generation 5: Generation 5 tags were introduced with a design that was dramatically different from the previously used red heart tag. The tag became beige with the front covered in tiny brown animal paw prints. The Ty logo became burgundy as did the "collectible" banner. The information on the inside is the same as previous generation tags. However, with the addition of clothing and other accessories with small buttons, an additional warning was added on the back of the tag. Here the words "Safety Precaution" appear above a specific advisement about the removal of "all tags, buttons, and other accessories before giving (the toy) to a child under 3 years of age."

Ty Collectibles ™
® Ty Inc.
Oakbrook. IL. U.S.A.
® Ty UK Ltd.
Fareham, Hants
PO15 5TX
® Ty Deutschland
90008 Nürnberg
Handmade in China

Mason ™ style 6020
Designed by Ruth E. Fraser
to _____
from _____
with
love

Generation 6: This design looks exactly like Generation 5 except that, on the inside, the style number has been deleted. This information can now be found on the back of the tag as the last four numbers of the UPC bar code. Also, the word "button" was removed in the "Safety Precaution" instructions.

The Attic Treasures Collection™
® Ty Inc.
Oakbrook. IL. U.S.A
® Ty Europe Ltd.
Fareham. Hants
PO15 5TX U.K.
® Ty Canada
Aurora. Ontario
Handmade in China

Piccadilly ™
to _____
from _____
with
love

Generation 7: In another dramatic tag change, Ty re-introduced the familiar red heart design for the *Attic Treasures Collection.* The front of the tag is adorned with the puffy "ty" letters. Inside, on the left, the information remains the same as that found on the Generation 6 tag. Major changes can be found, however, on the right side. This tag introduced the printing of a short phrase that further illustrates the animal's personality. Also, Ty's official company web site address appears for the first time. On the back of the tag, the information remains the same as Generation 6.

The Attic Treasures Collection™
® Ty Inc.
Oakbrook, IL. U.S.A.
® Ty Europe Ltd.
Fareham. Hants
PO15 5TX U.K.
® Ty Canada
Aurora. Ontario
Handmade in China

Jangle™
"Jingle All The Way !"
www.ty.com

Beanie Babies® Swing Tags

Generation 1 (Early 1994-Mid 1994): The first *Beanie Babies* were issued with red swing tags cut in the shape of a heart. These single sheet tags featured the Ty logo printed in a skinny font on the front, with the outside edge of the tag and the company name outlined in gold. The *Beanie Babies* name and style number were printed on the reverse side, as well as the collection name and relevant information.

> The Beanie Babies Collection
> Brownie ™ style 4010
> © 1993 Ty Inc. Oakbrook, IL. USA
> All Rights Reserved. Caution:
> Remove this tag before giving
> toy to a child. For ages 5 and up.
> Handmade in Korea.
> Surface
> Wash.

Generation 2 (Mid 1994-Early 1995): This newly designed tag opens like a book but carries the identical logo on the front as the Generation 1 tag. The *Beanie Babies* name, style number, company information, care and cautions are all found on the inside.

> The Beanie Babies Collection
> © 1993 Ty Inc. Oakbrook IL. USA
> All Rights Reserved, Caution:
> Remove this tag before giving
> toy to a child. For ages 3 and up.
> Handmade in China
> Surface
> Wash.
>
> Chilly ™ style 4012
> to _____
> from _____
> with
> love

Generation 3 (Early 1995-Early 1996): The Ty logo appears on this tag in a fat and puffy style. The inside information remains the same with the addition of a trademark symbol in the collection's name and Ty's three corporate addresses.

> The Beanie Babies ™ Collection
> © Ty Inc.
> Oakbrook IL. U.S.A.
> © Ty UK Ltd.
> Waterlooville, Hants
> PO8 8HH
> © Ty Deutschland
> 90008 Nürnberg
> Handmade in China
>
> Garcia ™ style 4051
> to _____
> from _____
> with
> love

Generation 4 (Early 1996-Late 1997): In the most dramatic change so far, a yellow star with the words "Original Beanie Baby" appears in the upper right-hand corner of the tag's front. Inside, the "to/from" section is replaced with the *Beanie's* birthday and poem and the company's official web site address.

> The Beanie Babies™ Collection
> © Ty Inc.
> Oakbrook IL. U.S.A.
> © Ty UK Ltd.
> Fareham, Hants
> PO15 5TX
> © Ty Deutschland
> 90008 Nürnberg
> Handmade in China
>
> Doodle™ style 4171
> DATE OF BIRTH : 3 - 8 - 96
> Listen closely to "cuck-a-doodle-doo"
> What's the rooster saying to you?
> Hurry, wake up sleepy head
> We have lots to do, get out of bed!
> Visit our web page!!!
> http://www.ty.com

SWING TAGS

Generation 5 (Late 1997–Current): At the end of 1997, the typeface of "Original Beanie Baby" printed on front, as well as the inside text was changed. The *Beanie's* birth date became written out, the Internet address abbreviated and the *Beanie's* style number moved to the last four digits of the UPC bar code on the back of the tag. The phrase "The Beanie Babies Collection" is now registered, the trademark symbol is dropped and the corporate offices are now collectively referred to as "Ty Europe."

The Beanie Babies Collection®

© Ty Inc.
Oakbrook, IL. U.S.A.
© Ty Europe Ltd.
Fareham, Hants
PO15 5TX, U.K.
© Ty Canada
Aurora, Ontario
Handmade in China

Pinky™

DATE OF BIRTH: February 13, 1995

Pinky loves the everglades
From the hottest pink she's made
With floppy legs and big orange beak
She's the Beanie that you seek!

www.ty.com

A New Generation?: During the summer of 1998, some *Beanie Babies* tags started appearing with slight differences. The writing in the star logo appeared with a different font and on the inside and the back of the tag, the font is larger and darker. Another slight change occurred a few months later when the Ty Europe Ltd. address was changed to "Gasport, Hampshire, U.K."

The Beanie Babies Collection®

© Ty Inc.
Oakbrook, IL. U.S.A.
© Ty Europe
Gasport, Hampshire, U.K.
© Ty Canada
Aurora, Ontario
Handmade in China

Goatee™

DATE OF BIRTH: November 4, 1998

Though she's hungry, she's in a good mood
Searching through garbage, tin cans for food
For Goatee the goat, it's not a big deal
Anything at all makes a fine meal!

www.ty.com

BEANIE BUDDIES® SWING TAGS

Generation 1: There has only been one generation of swing tags for this collection. The tag is the same size as the *Beanie Babies* tags and looks like a *Beanie Babies* 5th generation swing tag on the front, except the word "Buddy" appears instead of "Baby" in the yellow star. Inside, the tag has the name of the animal and a fact about its *Beanie Baby* counterpart.

The Beanie Buddies Collection®

© Ty Inc.
Oakbrook, IL. U.S.A.
© Ty Europe Ltd.
Fareham, Hants
PO15 5TX, U.K.
© Ty Canada
Aurora, Ontario
Handmade in China

Rover™

Rover the BEANIE BABY
was the first non-breed dog.
Introduced in the summer of 1996
this red color set him apart!

www.ty.com

TEENIE BEANIE BABIES™ SWING TAGS

1997 Version: The tags attached to this group of *Teenie Beanie Babies* are the single, non-folded type with the red, gold and white front design featuring the Ty logo with "puffy" lettering. On the tag's back, the name of the collection and the animal's name (both with the trademark symbols "TM/MC") are printed, as well as company information.

Teenie Beanie Babies ™/MC
Pinky™/MC   © Ty Inc.
                Oakbrook, IL
Printed in China
Imprimé en Chine

1998 Version: In this year's group of *Teenie Beanie Babies*, the front of the tag is the same, however the back of the tag now sports the official Ty web site address and a change in typeface. Additionally, the trademark symbols now read "TM/MC/MR." Slight spacing differences are also apparent due to multiple production sources.

Teenie Beanie Babies ™/MC/MR
Twigs ™/MC/MR   © Ty Inc.
                   Oakbrook, IL
www.ty.com
Printed in China
Imprimé en Chine

PILLOW PALS™ SWING TAGS

The *Pillow Pals* were originally introduced with large, red heart-shaped tags with the "puffed" Ty logo on the front and gold outlining the tag and the letters. This book-type tag has only the UPC bar code information on the back. On the inside left, "The Pillow Pals Collection," the company names and addresses and age suitability information are printed. On the right side, the piece's name and style number are listed above the "to/from/with love" section.

A smaller tag – the same size as the *Beanie Babies* tag – was then used with a front design identical to the previous tag. Inside, the care and age suitability information moved to the back of the tag and Ty's office locations were added to the com-

The Pillow Pals Collection®
© Ty Inc.
  Oakbrook, IL, U.S.A
© Ty Europe Ltd.
  Fareham, Hants
  PO15 5TX, U.K.
© Ty Canada
  Aurora, Ontario
Handmade in China

Sherbet™

Dear God, be with me as I start my day.
Please watch over me during school and play.

www.ty.com

SWING TAGS

pany information section. A subsequent design remained the same except the type font has changed and the style number moved from the inside to the back as the last four numbers of the bar code.

The Pillow Pals Collection®

© Ty Inc.
Oakbrook, IL. U.S.A.

© Ty Europe
Gasport, Hampshire, U.K.

© Ty Canada
Aurora, Ontario
Handmade in China

Meow™

As the day ends and turns to night,
Thank you God, for each twinkling light.

www.ty.com

Another new tag design appeared in 1998 with the "to/from/with love" section being replaced with prayer poems. This style tag has continued throughout 1998 and into 1999 with the most recent *Pillow Pal* releases.

Ty® PLUSH SWING TAGS

When Ty Inc. first introduced their plush line in 1986, a red, hard plastic heart tag was attached to the animal around its neck, but was discontinued when it was recognized as a safety hazard. There were several versions of the paper tag. A plain red heart tag with the letters "Ty" appears on some animals, while others have the same tag with the additional words "BEAN BAG" in red letters on a diagonal yellow banner in the upper right-hand corner.

© Ty Inc.
Oakbrook IL. U.S.A

© Ty Europe Ltd.
Fareham, Hants
P015 5TX

© Ty Canada
Aurora, Ontario
Handmade in Korea

Winston™·Style 2007

to _____

from _____

with
love

Later versions also appeared. The Ty logo appeared on the red tag in a horizontal fashion, with the letters "t" and "y" used as the first letters for the words "to" and "you," and the words "with love" written in script. Also, the tag design may also mirror the original Ty logo, except for the additional black border around the letters.

© Ty Inc.
Oakbrook. IL. U.S.A.

© Ty Europe Ltd.
Fareham, Hants
P015 5TX

© Ty Canada
Aurora. Ontario
Handmade in China

Churchill™

to _____

from _____

with

love

The current tag design features a larger, "puffed out" Ty logo. Two sizes of tags are used, depending on the size of the animal to which it is attached.

C hanges in design are also recognized in the cloth body tags (commonly referred to as "tush tags") that are sewn into the seam of Ty stuffed animals' posteriors. Although the information found on the tush tags can be helpful in determining the value and age of the item, this is not the most accurate strategy as even 1999 releases can have a 1993 date on their tush tag.

ATTIC TREASURES™ TUSH TAGS

The earliest *Attic Treasures* were introduced with tush tags that were white with black printing and had no Ty logo. Later, the tag design included the Ty heart on the white tag and the printing was in red. The current *Attic Treasures* tush tag is a distinctive burgundy color with the "Ty" name inside a white heart on front and cleaning instructions, company and content information listed on the back of the tush tag in white print.

BEANIE BABIES® TUSH TAGS

Version 1: Tush tags on the first *Beanie Babies* were white with black printing, listed the country in which it was produced and its contents.

Version 1

Version 2: The information on this version of the tush tag is printed in red and the red heart Ty logo was added.

Version 3: On this tag, the name of the *Beanie Baby* appears on the tag below the Ty heart while the words "The Beanie Babies Collection" are printed above the logo.

Version 4: This version of the tush tag features a small red star in the upper left-hand side of the Ty logo. On some tags, a clear sticker with the star was placed next to the logo.

Version 2   Version 3

TUSH TAGS

Version 4   Version 5

Version 6   Version 7

Version 5: By late 1997, these tags began to appear with a registration mark (®) after "The Beanie Babies Collection" title and a trademark symbol (™) after the animal's name.

Version 6: The 6th version of the *Beanie Babies* tush tag features a change in the placement of the trademark symbols. The registration mark in the collection's name moved from its position after the words "Beanie Babies" to after the word "Collection." A change in pellet content has also been noted. And in mid-1998, an oval, red stamp with numbers and Chinese writing has also been found on the inside of some *Beanie Baby* tush tags.

Version 7: The 1999 newly released *Beanie Babies* are now sporting a hologram on their tush tags. Within the silver rectangle, the words "The Beanie Babies Collection" can be found with two different designs underneath, depending on the angle at which the tag is viewed. On the back of the tush tag a "disappearing" red Ty heart logo is printed behind the text. It vanishes upon being touched!

BEANIE BUDDIES® TUSH TAGS

Version 1   Version 2

Version 1: The tush tags of the first *Beanie Buddies* were white with a red heart containing the word "ty" in white letters. The back of the tag provides the company name and fabric information in black writing.

Version 2: The current *Beanie Buddy* tush tags are printed entirely in red and the words "The Beanie Buddies Collection®" appears above the distinctive red Ty heart logo.

TEENIE BEANIE BABIES™ TUSH TAGS

The tush tags on the *Teenie Beanie Babies* feature the red Ty heart, company and production information and date of copyright printed in red. On the reverse side, printed in black above the content information, the first line names the manufacturing company – either Simon Marketing of Los Angeles, California or M-B Sales of Westmont, Illinois.

PILLOW PALS™ TUSH TAGS

The tush tags on the original *Pillow Pals* display the red Ty heart on one side and, on the other side, a listing of Ty company information as well as age and care recommendations. Eventually, the information concerning age recommendation was eliminated and the "CE" symbol was added.

TY® PLUSH TUSH TAGS

The Ty tush tags are sometimes the only identifying symbol on a stuffed animal of unknown origin, especially on the older toys who have lost their paper swing tags. The *Ty Plush* tush tag has gone through several variations throughout the years. An early version was a cream satin tag with a red heart outline surrounding the letters "ty" written in black. More recent pieces feature a white tush tag with a red Ty heart logo on the front. On the reverse side, "Ty, Inc." and the copyright year appear in red type, with company and production information in dark brown or black type. The text varies on these tags, including pellet information (P.V.C or P.E) and country of production (China or Korea).

PROTECTING AND INSURING YOUR COLLECTION

𝒫rotecting a collection of stuffed animals requires a different approach, for example, than when protecting a collection of fragile crystal. Ty plush animals were originally and continue to be marketed as children's toys. This means that they've been designed to be played with, slept with and loved by little fingers. Consequently, the

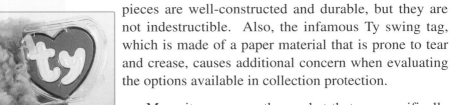

pieces are well-constructed and durable, but they are not indestructible. Also, the infamous Ty swing tag, which is made of a paper material that is prone to tear and crease, causes additional concern when evaluating the options available in collection protection.

Many items are on the market that are specifically designed to protect the swing tag on your plush animal. Varying designs offer many choices, but any clear, acrylic cover that snaps on or slides over the entire tag will provide protection from tearing and folding.

To preserve the animal in its "mint" condition, collectors have become very creative and have come up with a number of effective ways to safeguard its appearance. Many acrylic containers in a variety of shapes and sizes have permeated the market in an effort to provide options to collectors. In addition to providing protection, these boxes also have become a space-saving way to store the animals. Some collectors also use large, plastic storage boxes or bins to protect their animals, especially when transporting a collection to shows or swap & sells. Another way to protect a stuffed animal is to use inexpensive, plastic storage bags that have airtight closures which can be convenienetly purchased at your local grocery store!

For Ty plush animal lovers who buy these irresistible critters to cuddle and kiss, an occasional dip in the tub is a periodic aesthetic requirement. The *Pillow Pals* and the

Protecting And Insuring Your Collection

majority of the *Beanie Babies* are machine-washable, but those with glued-on or felt appendages and/or features should be spot-washed. Before exposing your animal to the sudsy depths of your washing machine, the paper swing tag should be removed and the animal placed inside a pillow case, which should be tied shut with a shoestring or similar fastener. A mild detergent should be used in a gentle wash cycle. Let your animal air dry or use your hair dryer on the cool setting to fluff the fur!

Ty Plush, *Attic Treasures* and *Beanie Buddies* require more care in the cleaning process. *Ty Plush* and *Attic Treasures* pieces specify on their tags that surface cleaning is recommended. A damp washcloth dipped in a mild detergent can be rubbed on the dirty area but testing on a hidden area first for fading should be done to assure colorfastness of the fur or material. A method that is often used to remove offensive odors from plush animals is to place it in a closed container with an open box of baking soda. Any odors should disappear within 24 hours.

Although collectors take exhaustive measures to protect their collection, accidents can happen! Insurance for a large, valuable collection is advisable. Most renters and homeowners insurance policies cover collectibles, however, an additional Personal Articles or a Fine Arts Floater, or "rider," policy can ensure cost replacement in case of accidental loss.

INSURANCE POLICY

An accurate record of your collection's content and value is necessary if you ever have to make a claim. To determine the type and amount of coverage you will need, calculate the total replacement cost of your collection and compare the amount with the cost of the policy and what it would pay. Weigh your options and make decisions wisely!

GLOSSARY

CE — mark imprinted on tush tags of Ty plush animals, indicating that the pieces were manufactured according to consumer safety regulations.

COLLECTIBLE — anything and everything that is "able to be collected," such as figurines and dolls. Even *sugar packets* can be considered a "collectible," but it is generally recognized that a true collectible should be something that increases in value over time.

CURRENT — a piece that is in current production and available in retail stores.

INFO BEANIE — a *Beanie Baby* character who is elected to narrate the *Beanie Babies'* daily activities through a diary found on the Ty web site. A new "Info Beanie" is chosen each month by collectors who visit the site.

ISSUE PRICE — the original retail price of an item.

ISSUE YEAR — the year that a piece becomes available in the general collection.

LIMITED EDITION (LE) — piece scheduled for a predetermined production quantity or time.

MARKINGS — any of the various identifying features found on a collectible. This can be information found on tush tags or swing tags, such as an artist's signature.

MEMBERS-ONLY PIECE — special pieces only available for purchase by members of the Beanie Babies Official Club. In 1998, the members-only piece was "Clubby."

MINT CONDITION — piece offered on the secondary market that is in like-new condition.

MINT CONDITION WITH BOTH TAGS (MWBT) — piece offered on the secondary market in like-new condition with pristine swing tag and tush tag attached.

MINT IN BAG (MIB) — on the secondary market, the term used for *Teenie Beanie Babies* in like-new condition in the original, unopened plastic bag.

MISTAGS — errors in swing tags and tush tags, including mismatched tags and misspellings. Because Ty plush animals are mass produced, tag errors are common and rarely affect a piece's value of the secondary market.

NEW RELEASE — new piece in the collection announced during the year. For Ty plush animals, there are usually two or three major introductions per year.

OPEN EDITION — piece with no pre-determined limitation on time or size of production run.

P.E. PELLETS — small, round plastic polyethylene "beans" used as weighted fillings in many Ty plush animals.

PRIMARY MARKET — conventional collectibles purchasing process in which collectors buy directly from dealers at issue price.

P.V.C. PELLETS — small round plastic polyvinyl chloride "beans" used as weighted fillings in many Ty plush animals.

RETIRED — a piece that is taken out of production, never to be made again. This is usually followed by a scarcity of the piece and an increase in value on the secondary market.

SECONDARY MARKET — the source for buying and selling collectibles according to basic supply-and-demand principles ("pay what the market will bear"). Popular pieces that are sold out or have been retired can appreciate in value far above the original issue price. Pieces are sold through newspaper ads, collector newsletters, the Internet and swap & sells at collector gatherings.

SWAP & SELL — secondary market event where collectors meet to buy, sell or trade items.

SWING TAG — heart-shaped paper tag that comes attached to each Ty plush animal. This tag is attached by a small plastic strip, and is usually attached to the animal's left ear or head area.

© 1993 TY INC.,
OAKBROOK IL.
MADE IN CHINA

TAG GENERATIONS — style changes in the swing tags, which can help determine the approximate age of Ty plush animals.

TUSH TAG — folded fabric tag sewn into the seam near the bottom of the Ty plush animal (note: *Teenie Beanie Babies* do not have folded tags).

SIMON MARKETING INC.
LOS ANGELES, CA.
ALL NEW MATERIALS
CONTENTS: POLYESTER
FIBERS, HDPE PELLETS
REG NO. PA-6692 (HK)
© 1996 McDonald's Corp.
MADE IN CHINA CR2

TYLON — a special fabric developed by Ty Warner himself for *Beanie Buddies*. This fabric is very soft and cool to the touch.

VARIATIONS — items that have color, design or printed text changes from the "original" piece, whether intentional or not. Some of these changes are minor, while some are important enough to affect the value of a piece on the secondary market.

– Key –

All Ty plush animals are listed below in order by animal types. The first number refers to the piece's location (Page #) in the book and the second number refers to the box (Pict #) in which it is pictured on that page.

Attic Treasures™ — (AT)
Beanie Babies® — (BB)
Beanie Buddies® — (BU)
Teenie Beanie Babies™ — (TB)
Pillow Pals™ — (PP)
Ty® Plush — (PL)

INDEX BY ANIMAL TYPE

ALPHABETICAL INDEX

– Key –

All Ty plush animals are listed below in alphabetical order. The first number refers to the piece's location (Page #) in the book and the second number refers to the box (Pict #) in which it is pictured on that page.

Attic Treasures™ — (AT)
Beanie Babies® — (BB)
Beanie Buddies® — (BU)
Teenie Beanie Babies™ — (TB)
Pillow Pals™ — (PP)
Ty® Plush — (PL)

ALPHABETICAL INDEX

ACKNOWLEDGEMENTS

CheckerBee Publishing would like to thank Leslie Foucher, Shana L. Foucher, Ellen Hearst, Adam Majowicz, Wendy Murray, Jennifer Smolin, Michele Smolin and all of the Ty retailers and collectors who contributed their valuable time to assist us with this book.

Ty® Beanie
Babies®

Ty® Plush
Animals

BOYDS BEARS & FRIENDS™

The
BOYDS COLLECTION LTD

Charming
Tails

Cherished
Teddies®
by ENESCO®

Department 56®
Snowbabies™

Department 56®
Villages

Dreamsicles®

HALLMARK
Keepsake Ornaments

HARBOUR
LIGHTS

PRECIOUS
MOMENTS
by ENESCO

SWAROVSKI
Silver Crystal

Look for these

COLLECTOR'S
VALUE GUIDE™

TITLES AT **FINE GIFT** AND
COLLECTIBLE STORES EVERYWHERE

FEATURING

❯ **What's New**
❯ **Full-Color Photos Of Every Piece**
❯ **Easy-To-Use Tabs & Indexes**
❯ **Up-To-Date Secondary Market Values**

Visit our web site

www.
collectorbee.com

FOR ALL OF THE
LATEST COLLECTIBLES NEWS

CheckerBee
PUBLISHING

306 Industrial Park Road | **Middletown, CT 06457**